LABRADOR RETRIEVER

FROM THE EDITORS OF DOGFANCY MAGAZINE

CONTENTS

Labrador Retriever, a Smart Owner's Guide™
part of the Kennel Club Books® Interactive Series™
ISBN: 978-1-593787-67-7. ©2009
Kennel Club Books Inc., 40 Broad St., Freehold, NJ 07728. Printed in South Korea. All rights reserved.
No part of this book may be reproduced in any form, by Photostat, scanner, microfilm, xerography, or any other means, or incorporated into any information retrieval system, electronic or mechanical, without the written permission of the copyright owner.

photographers include Tara Darling, Isabelle Français, Carol Ann Johnson, Alice van Kempen and Alice Pantfoeder

K9 EXPERT

Congratulations! If you are considering adding a Labrador Retriever to your home, you are the newest member of a huge and very enthusiastic fan club. The Lab is the most popular dog breed in America, and what's not to like? Handsome, sturdy, and easy to care for, the Lab's devotion to his family is legendary.

Whether he is leaping into an ice-cold pond to retrieve waterfowl, performing as an indispensable guide dog to the blind, carrying out grueling search-and-rescue maneuvers, or simply stretched out at your feet as you read the newspaper or watch TV, the Lab's long history of working in the service of mankind is an illustrious one. He wants nothing more than to serve you in whatever capacity he can.

While there are breeds with food issues, complicated grooming regimens, and quirky behavioral challenges, the Lab is nothing if not an easy keeper. He is intelligent yet sensible, with a hearty appetite and a spirited sense of humor; definitely not a candidate for the doggie psychiatrist's couch. Happily, most Lab owners are as easygoing and low maintenance as their dogs.

Despite the breed's popularity, there is nothing glamorous, exotic, or exaggerated about the Lab. He is a handy size for most city and suburban homes with a fenced backyard. The Lab is the perfect jogging companion for active singles as well as a loving, robust pet for children. Of course, bred for endurance in the field and water, he must be given sufficient exercise or his love of food will soon catch up with him. This is no discriminating gourmet who will turn down a free meal. In fact, you'd better keep those cupboard doors securely closed or he'll be rummaging around for unscheduled feedings. Did we say he was an easy keeper? That's a

euphemism for chow hound! And those extra pounds will put an added strain on his heart, hips, and joints. The Lab is an athlete and a field champ. He shouldn't look like a watermelon on legs!

The American Kennel Club breed standard recognizes three acceptable colors for the breed: glossy black, rich chocolate, and shades of yellow ranging from light cream to deep fox red. Notice that we didn't say "white" or "silver." White is basically a pale, pale cream while silver is not even mentioned in the standard. Steer clear of breeders who hype these "rare" and "unusual" colors in their advertising, hoping to reel in an unsuspecting novice. The Lab has far too many wonderful qualities to fixate on color. No serious dog owner buys a dog to match the color of the living-room sofa.

Whichever color you prefer, a quick grooming several times a week with a brush or hound mitt will remove dead hair before it ends up on your floors and carpets, and will keep him gleaming. Ears and eyes will need to be cleaned as well, and his nails trimmed. But that's it. No doggie salon needed for this sporting dude.

If you've watched agility, rally, or dock dogs (a long-distance diving competition) on TV and think you might want to give it a try, your Lab will be an enthusiastic partner. If you prefer to swim, rollerblade, or jog, he's happy keeping you company during those activities, as well. At the end of the day, he'll sack out to watch a movie with you, or curl up under your desk, thumping his tail against your leg as you answer e-mails. Labs are all about the bonding; the activity is always negotiable.

JOIN OUR ONLINE **Lab Club**

With this Smart Owner's Guide™, you are well on your way to getting your Labrador diploma. But your Labrador Retriever education doesn't end here. You're invited to join Club Lab™ (**DogChannel.com/Club-Lab**), a FREE online site with lots of fun and instructive online features like:

- ◆ **forums, blogs,** and **profiles** where you can connect with other Lab owners
- ◆ **downloadable charts** and **checklists** to help you be a smart and loving Labrador Retriever owner
- ◆ access to **e-cards, wallpapers,** and **screensavers**
- ◆ interactive **games**
- ◆ Lab-specific **quizzes**

The **Smart Owner's Guide**™ series and Club Lab™ are backed by the experts at DOG FANCY magazine and DogChannel.com—who have been providing trusted and up-to-date information about dogs and dog people for forty years. Log on and join the club today!

You could not find a sweeter, more loving or more versatile breed than the Lab. One look into his kind, friendly eyes will reassure you that you chose wisely. The AKC Lab standard states that "… good temperament, intelligence and alertness are a hallmark." How do you top those three great qualities?

Allan Reznik
Editor-at-Large, DOG FANCY

The answer to the question "Why the Labrador Retriever?" too often seems to be "Why not!" Because there are literally millions of happy Labrador lovers around the world, why shouldn't everyone love a Lab? Given the breed's good looks, trainability, loyalty, and intelligence, why isn't this the dog for everyone on the planet who loves dogs?

Let's begin by listing the kinds of people who should not consider the ubiquitous Labrador for their lives.

Lap-Dog Lookers: The Lab is no lap dog. Sure, he'll want to "lap" and kiss you constantly, but he's too big to sit on your lap while you're reading or spending time in front of the television. Labradors like to be close to you, that's for sure, but 60 pounds (or more) of true love is too much for anyone's lap!

Couch Potatoes: Labradors love to romp and play, preferably with their trusted owners close by. Because the breed is designed for chasing birds in the swamp or swimming toward fallen ducks, Labs most definitely have energy to spare. Most pet Labrador owners do not have the time or inclination to take their dogs out on weekend duck hunts,

it's a Fact

In 1830, the 2nd Earl of Malmesbury imported what might have been the first St. John's or Labrador dogs to England. He unloaded the dogs at Poole Harbor, Dorset, in southern England.

Labs are very active, and need activities to keep them busy.

so Labradors will need other outlets for their abundant energy.

No Boundaries: The Lab needs a sizeable piece of property on which to exercise, and a fence is imperative. As a gundog, the Labrador does not have a strong sense of territory, and he will not guard his property the way a Rottweiler or Doberman Pinscher will.

This is not to say that he is not protective—he is most protective of his family and home. However, if not fenced in, he will more likely tear off in pursuit of a flapping pigeon than stay close by and stand watch.

Outdoor Only: The Labrador Retriever, for all his natural good looks and charm, does not fancy an owner who doesn't want to get up close to him and spend time with him indoors and out. Like most of the sporting breeds, the Labrador likes to be near his family. While it is true that the Labrador's ancestors were "kennel dogs," today's Lab is strongly inclined to be indoors with his master and loved ones. To keep a Labrador Retriever outdoors exclusively will be torture to the poor dog, and such owners should consider a different breed or no dog at all. While the breed is renowned for its adapt-ability with any lifestyle, the breed is best when kept indoors and given time to spend outdoors. A happy Labrador is the true Labrador, and close to you is where he will want to be.

Neatniks: The Labrador sheds. Even though the breed has a short, dense coat, he does not cast coat any less than any other dog. Furthermore, the Lab is not, as a

rule, a genteel or docile animal—he's a "doggie" dog, and he likes to play inside and out. Owners will have to enforce the house rules immediately with the puppy, or else he may think he can roughhouse inside the house and out. Labradors can be raucous, rambunctious, and rowdy—that's three "Rs" potential owners may have to live with.

ARE YOU A LABRADOR PERSON?

For all the talents of Labrador Retrievers, the breed is still only canine. That is to say, the Labrador is not a superdog. Mary Feazell, a Labrador fancier and trainer, contends that ninety-five percent of what a Labrador can grow up to be depends upon the owner; only five percent depends on the dog itself. That's a huge responsibil-ity for the owner of this fabulously talented dog! There is little that a Labrador cannot learn. Some Labs recognize hundreds of words and can execute dozens of com-mands. Feazell says, "Being realistic, Labs swim well, but they can't walk on water."

A Labrador Retriever requires a smart and dedicated owner, whether the pursuit is basic obedience (such as sit, stay, come, and lie down, the cues necessary for a well-trained home companion), or more lofty pur-suits like obedience trials, field trials, agility trials, and working trials. Many Labs are so intelligent and have such a strong desire to please that they become self-trained.

Labradors are excellent problem-solvers and quickly decide what pleases their mas-

ters and what does not! Such self-learned abilities include coming when called, staying where he's put, not bolting through the front door every time it is opened, not jumping up on visitors, permitting people to pet and touch him, and not messing in the house.

Labrador Retrievers are smart, but you must be there to show the dog right from wrong. This is no different from instructing a child. Parents must be present for their children if they are to mature properly.

Absent parents do not discipline, teach, or help their children. Likewise, Labs must receive enough training to make them capable of self-control and amenable to obeying cues, and minding their owners' wishes.

The smart owner controls what kind of dog his Labrador becomes. The owner provides the dog with training, guidance, encouragement, and outlets for his energy and industry. The Lab who doesn't have proper parental guidance can develop

Labs make great family dogs because they love everyone, especially children.

behavioral problems, including destructive habits, aggression, and fear-biting, to name a few. The owner molds his Labrador into the dog with whom he wants to live.

Investing time, money, and love into a dog can pay off a thousandfold; skimping on the time and education that a dog as active and bright as a Labrador requires can be an owner's worst mistake. Do not rush into becoming a Labrador owner. This is a breed that deserves a smart owner, and if you're not sure about the acquisition, delay your decision. Read more about the breed; talk to breeders, owners, and trainers; attend a dog show; and meet people who commit their lives to their dogs. Then, you'll be better prepared to know whether you're ready to dive into dog ownership.

For those of you who are certain that a Labrador Retriever is the dog with whom you want to share your life, this wonderful dog can become your world. Whether it's a pet companion dog, show dog or field and working dog you require, the Labrador Retriever can become all you want in a faithful canine friend.

Labs require daily or weekly brushing, depending on the time of year and the amount of shedding. In addition, their grooming schedule includes weekly nail clipping and an ear/nose/eye check. Lab puppies do not need to be bathed as often as people sometimes think. Their smell comes from the sweating of their paw pads, and simply wiping the feet

it's a
Fact

Although the Lab's hunting heritage can give him prodigious levels of energy, another aspect of that heritage—the breed's short coat— is advantageous to a busy owner. The Lab was bred with short fur because longer coats would freeze up after emerging from cold water, and this no-freeze coat makes the dog relatively easy to groom.

regularly can significantly reduce odor. Because the coat will shed dirt, grime, and oils regularly, a Lab puppy only needs a bath every three to four weeks.

Labrador Retrievers are good with many types of animals. The younger your Lab is when he is introduced to other animals, the more accepting he will be of them when he gets older. Lab puppies can live harmo-niously with cats, rabbits, ferrets, guinea pigs, and other dogs.

Labs are great with children. Before you bring your Lab home, be sure to teach your child the appropriate way to approach, play with, call, and hold a Lab puppy. Use stuffed animals for younger children to practice with. You can teach your child to approach slowly with back of the hand extended; sit on the floor and hold the puppy in the lap; never to pull the dog's ears or tail; and to pet the puppy gently. Show your child how to gently push a puppy down if the puppy jumps up, and how to calmly react if a puppy gets rowdy or overly playful. That way, your child will be prepared to deal with the real thing once you bring your new puppy home.

Labrador Retrievers require training, and the younger he starts, the better. If he can start puppy kindergarten before six months of age, then follow up with beginning and intermediate classes, he will have a good foundation. The trainer will be able to identify problem areas for your puppy during this time, and will be able to head off any possible bad habits before your Lab puppy reaches adulthood.

The Labrador Retriever coat colors are black, yellow, and chocolate. Any other color or a combination of colors is a disqualification in the show ring, according to the breed standard. A small white spot on the chest is permissible, however, but not desirable.

Black—Blacks should be all black.

Yellow—Yellows may range in color from fox-red to light cream, with variations in shading on the ears, back and underparts of the dog.

Chocolate—Chocolates can vary in shade from light to dark chocolate.

Labs come in three colors: black, yellow and chocolate.

This breed loves to do all the things that his family does.

Labs are notorious chewers. They will chew and eat all kinds of things, both edible and inedible. Some of these things can be harmful or even deadly, so confining your puppy to an acceptable radius by using baby gates or a crate can help keep him safe.

Labs love to swim and play in water. Lab puppies can be exposed to water as soon as they are up and running around, and cer-tainly by eight weeks of age, when they are typically allowed to leave the breeder.

A fenced yard is almost always a neces-sity, and different kinds of fencing can work for your puppy. The important qualities of the fence are height and security. Labradors are good at jumping, climbing up and over, and digging under fences. They are excellent at learning to open gates. Place a secure lock on whatever containment you choose, anchor the bottom of chain-link fencing, and if using an outdoor run, buy one with an enclosed top.

HE'S A PEOPLE PERSON

Although the Labrador Retriever is bred to hunt and retrieve, he does not do so alone. These tasks require him to work closely with a human partner. Consequently, Labs are born extroverts. They have strong social instincts and are eager to please the human members of their packs.

This sociability makes Labs easy to train and happy to participate in any activity you'd like to do with them. However, the Lab's outgoing nature has a flip side. Although Labs have great temperaments, they truly crave, demand, and deserve lots of attention. This will not be a breed to leave home alone all day, come home from work, and go out again at night. They can become very depressed and may take out their frustrations through destructive behavior aimed at your home or self-mutilation like excessive foot chewing or leg licking.

Fortunately, Labrador Retrievers are not only sociable but also versatile. The breed's generally sunny disposition, love of people, and willingness to learn make these dogs star performers in many disciplines. They're field dogs, companion dogs, therapy dogs; they're all-around good dogs. They are incredibly adaptable.

People underestimate the amount a correctly coated Lab can shed. At least twice a year, a Lab will shed his coat. You will find hair everywhere from the car seats to the fireplace mantle to the lampshades. The more you brush your Lab, the less you will have to vacuum.

—Laura Dedering of Bangor, Pa..

LABS ARE ACTIVE

Labrador Retrievers have to be active to accompany a hunter from dawn to dusk, running, swimming, and retrieving. That high energy level is great for active people who like to run, swim, and play fetch. But it can be disastrous for people who like to sit, relax, and watch television. These inactive people often label their dogs as hyperactive, but the dogs are really just doing what they were bred to do.

Most people say they want an energetic dog. In today's society, it's good to be athletic, and few people openly admit that a they want a dog that matches their sedentary, inactive lifestyle. People also tend to overestimate the time they can devote to a dog, and as the excitement of playing with a new puppy subsides, the dog may be left to entertain himself.

Adult Labrador Retrievers need thirty to sixty minutes of interactive exercise every morning and evening. You can't just put a Lab in the yard while you're cooking dinner because Labs tend not to exercise themselves—at least not in constructive ways. They may bark, chew, and dig, but most owners interpret that as unruly behavior, not exercise. Labs only get appropriate exercise when it is directed by a person, either by walking, hiking, swimming, or retrieving. Don't think bad weather is an excuse to take the day off; the

Lab adults almost never lose that play- ful quality they pos- sess when they're puppies.

typical Lab thinks a hurricane only makes the outing more invigorating. Water is fun!

ORALLY ORIENTED

Labrador Retrievers were developed to use their jaws like a strong and dexterous hand. In the absence of birds to retrieve, they'll mouth and carry just about anything in reach. That's great for people who like to play fetch or compete in advanced obedience competitions. It's bad for those who don't give their Labradors an outlet for his need to carry and manipulate objects in his mouth.

This oral fixation leads to a complaint common among Lab owners. This inclination to hold things in the mouth often includes human arms and hands. The Lab's oral fixation can lead to health problems such as obesity or ingesting foreign objects or poisons.

Labs are mouthy dogs, meaning they love to chew, lick, nibble, and gnaw.

Why does the Labrador Retriever consistently rank as the most-registered breed in America, the United Kingdom, and Canada?

1. Labs are incredibly photogenic. The yellows are easiest to photograph.

2. Labs are their own best ambassadors. People meet or hear of other people's Labradors and hope to get one just like them.

3. The easygoing Lab is especially patient with children. The only problem he poses is that in his enthusiastic jumping, the Lab may accidentally knock over a child. Teaching your Lab not to jump on people or items will prevent this problem.

4. Labs love water. What breed is better to take to the beach or the lake?

5. Labs are incredibly versatile. These dogs excel at pursuits such as conformation, obedience, field trials, assistance to the handicapped, and therapy work. This versatility will come in handy when you and your Labrador Retriever confront new situations. What may seem difficult to you may not be a big deal to your Lab.

6. If brushing a long-coated dog like a Golden Retriever or an Afghan Hound isn't your thing, look to the Lab. His short coat makes grooming easy: A fast weekly brushing and nail trim, and periodic ear cleanings are all that's needed—and you can perform those tasks at home. There's no need to pay a grooming pro.

7. Labs are a good-size dog but not so big that an adult would have trouble dealing with one. Put another way: Their height makes them just right for petting.

8. The Lab loves everyone and anyone, and is never shy about demonstrating his affection. If the aloof natures of some northern breeds like Siberian Huskies or Alaskan Malamutes don't appeal to you, look no further than a Lab.

9. Unlike some other breeds, such as Shetland Sheepdogs, Beagles, and Welsh Corgis, the Lab doesn't need to hear himself talk. Labradors bark only when there's a reason, such as notifying the household that someone's at the door.

10. They love life. The exuberant, adaptable Lab has much to teach human beings about how to enjoy being alive.

RETRIEVER REPORT

This friendly, sporty breed has won the hearts of dog owners the world over.

COUNTRY OF ORIGIN: Canada

WHAT HIS FRIENDS CALL HIM: Lab

SIZE: males—22½ to 24½ inches tall (measured to the withers, aka shoulders), 65 to 80 pounds; females—21½ to 23½ inches, 55 to 70 pounds

COAT & COLOR: short, straight, dense, double coat that can be either yellow, black, or chocolate in color

PERSONALITY TRAITS: adaptable, affectionate, personable, versatile, intelligent. Labs were originally bred to assist hunters retrieving water birds, but they continue to help people by serving in the fields of therapy, drug- and arson-detecting, and assisting people with disabilities.

WITH KIDS: excellent with children. Labrador Retrievers are people pooches and love everyone, including young children.

WITH OTHER PETS: good with other dogs and most other pets

ENERGY LEVEL: high

EXERCISE NEEDS: Labs are energetic and love to play and work hard. A daily walk is a must, as well as regular play sessions. Labs have a tendency to become overweight, so daily activity is essential for the breed.

GROOMING NEEDS: Labrador Retrievers shed occasionally, so they must be combed and brushed regularly with a firm-bristled brush, making sure to get all the way to the undercoat.

TRAINING NEEDS: Intelligent and eager to please, Labs are easily trained, especially when lessons are coupled with toys or treats. All Labs should be taught the five basics cues: sit, lie down, stay, come and heel.

LIVING ENVIRONMENT: Though Labs will adapt to almost any area, they do best in a rural or suburban environment with a fenced yard.

LIFESPAN: 10 to 14 years

BREED HISTORY

What introduction does the world's most popular dog require? Everyone has seen a Labrador Retriever romping happily with his family. Regarded as the ideal family dog for generations, the Labrador is by definition biddable and adaptable to practically any lifestyle.

It's common today to hear the breed simply referred to as the Labrador; however, they are much more than that. The Labrador is a retriever. The Labrador Retriever, a prominent member of the American Kennel Club's Sporting Group, is a hunting dog by trade. The pet Labrador Retriever comes from a lineage of hard-working hunters who could spend tireless hours tracking upland game birds on rigorous terrain. While your Labrador Retriever may only fetch your slippers and the Sunday paper, it is helpful to understand that his predecessors pursued pheasant, duck, and other wild fowl.

Well, that's the "retriever" part of his name; what's the meaning of the "Labrador" part? To understand the breed's origins, we must look not to the region of Labrador in northeastern Canada, but to the island off its southern shores: Newfoundland. The rich

Did You Know?

Pres. Bill Clinton had a chocolate Labrador named Buddy, who arrived in 1997 to live in the White House. Clinton famously quipped, "If you want a friend in Washington, you have to get a dog."

history of this island, originally inhabited by the Dorset Eskimos, dates back to the 1400s; however, it wasn't until the 1600s that the island became the home of wayward fishermen. These fishermen, it is believed, swam to the island after abandoning ships that were passing by the island. As these fishermen tended to be free spirits, the island went without laws or establishments of any kind for the next two centuries.

The first dogs on the island of Newfoundland are traced to these fishermen because there is no evidence of the Eskimos' having dogs on the island, and no dogs existed on Newfoundland when the fishermen landed there. As the Labrador Retriever was once called the Lesser Newfoundland Dog, it has often been presumed that the breed is related to the Newfoundland breed. The Newfoundland, however, is a much larger, more abundantly coated, heavy-boned dog, showing much influence of its mastiff origins. Still, the Newfoundland and the Labrador Retriever share the unique physical characteristic of webbed feet.

The island of Newfoundland has terrain and weather conditions that are rugged, requiring a dog of surefootedness, stamina, and buoyancy. The size of the Labrador Retriever was important because the dogs had to fit into the fishermen's dories. The dogs' webbed feet speak well for the Lab's ability to swim, even in the icy, rough waters of the North Atlantic. Among the other char-

acteristics of our modern Labrador that make sense for a dog surviving on Newfoundland's brutal shores is his thick and waterproof coat. The breed's broad chest helped Labs "surf" against the strong waves and current of the unrelenting North Atlantic. The island was bountiful in game, so the fishermen were able to use their dogs to supplement

their food supply from the land as well as from the sea.

The Newfoundlanders were importing quality retriever stock from England, though there was considerable variation in type. At this time (circa 1780 to 1810), any retriever—long-haired, curly-coated, short-coated, wavy-coated—was bred to produce other retrievers of excellent working ability. The division of the retriever breeds did not come until much later.

Labradors weren't the only dogs on the island at this point, as settlers brought other types; however, as the reputation of the Lab grew, these other types were often replaced with Labradors. Because the Labrador Retriever's disposition and adaptability were so highly respected, hunters and sportsmen deemed them the dogs of choice. The retrievers soon replaced the pointers and setters that had stood beside these sportsmen. Although the Labrador Retriever we know today comes in three acceptable colors—black, yellow, and chocolate—the dogs on Newfoundland were principally black. These small, black dogs were sometimes referred to as St. John's Water Dogs and were called "the best of any kind of dog for shooting...by far."

A frustrating fact to Labrador Retriever enthusiasts today is that the residents of Newfoundland kept no records of the dogs on which they relied so heavily. Survival on this barren island was such an all-encompassing pursuit that there was little time for recordkeeping.

it's a Fact

In 1959, a black Labrador Retriever named King Buck was the first dog to appear on a U.S. postage stamp.

THE LABRADOR COMES TO BRITAIN

The second and third Earls of Malmesbury are credited for exporting the famous St. John's Dogs from Newfoundland to Great Britain. The dogs at this point in time (around 1825) were sometimes called Little Newfoundlers. The third Earl, the pioneer breeder of these dogs, is credited with changing the breed's name to Labrador Retriever. These gentry and others like them kept the Labradors pure, breeding them only to dogs imported from Newfoundland, as they were exceptional in their swimming, retrieving, and fighting abilities. It is also said that any of the puppies from these St. John's Dogs that were crossed to other dogs usually maintained the strong appearance of the Labrador—black, short fur, a noncurling tail, and webbed feet. As early as the 1870s,

Labs are prized dogs because they are pleasant, hard-working, and sturdy.

the breed was described as symmetrical and elegant, and the temperament was praised and considered a requirement for the utility of the Labrador. It's no doubt that these early breeders' commitment to a sound disposition in the Labrador Retriever contributed to the breed's forthcoming popularity around the world as a great family dog.

In 1903, the Labrador Retriever was recognized by England's Kennel Club. Later that year, the breed was listed separately as a member of the Gundog Group. The retrievers at this point were still not divided by breed as they are today. It was not until early 1905, when the Labrador Retriever was separately listed, that The Kennel Club began to differ-

JOIN OUR ONLINE Lab Club

You have an unbreakable bond with your dog, but do you always understand him? Go online and download "Dog Speak," which outlines how dogs communicate. Find out what your Lab is saying when he barks, howls, or growls. Go to **DogChannel.com/Club-Lab** and click on "downloads."

Water lovers by nature, Labs excel at anything where they're paddling their webbed feet.

entiate between retriever "breeds." There is confusion in the records from these early days because some dogs were called "golden" and others "Labrador," though there is no indication about coat length. Thus, those "Golden Retrievers" may have indeed been yellow Labrador Retrievers. This was the early days of purebred dog enthusiasm. As a rule, a yellow Labrador is never called a "golden" Labrador.

The Kennel Club's stud books contain references to liver-colored, wavy-coated retrievers. These dogs trace back to the chocolate Labrador Retrievers of the famous Buccleuch Kennels, the breeders responsible for six of the first seven retrievers entered in the stud book. Buccleuch Kennels produced the famous field trial champion by

the name of Peter of Faskally, who is known to be behind many of the top Labradors from the early days as well as many of the top field dogs in England and the United States. Many of the early breed books still in print depict these famous dual champions—that is, dogs titled as both a bench (show) champion and a field trial champion.

The best yellow Labs are traced back to a dog by the name of Ben of Hyde, who was whelped in 1899. He was bred to many excellent black females, and his genes were passed on to the top yellow Lab kennels throughout England. Black Labs were most abundant until the period after World War II, which marked an increase in the popularity of yellow Labs.

Lorna Howe, along with Lord Knutsford, founded the U.K.'s Labrador Club in 1916 and held the first field trial there in 1920. Lord Knutsford authored the first Labrador Retriever breed standard in 1923, which is a written description of the ideal specimen of the breed. Knutsford's standard has changed very little to the present day. Countess Howe, considered the greatest of Labrador breed-

it's a
Fact

In 1899, the first recorded yellow Lab, named Ben of Hyde, was born. He was from the kennel of Major C.J. Radclyffe in England.

Meet Sadie: Accelerant Detector Dog

It had been an intense, fast fire that even when hit with water, continued to flash up—a red flag among firefighters that an accelerant, such as gasoline, had been used to purposely set the fire.

At 1 a.m. a call was made for the accelerant-detector dog to come by.

When Jesse Storey, certified fire investigator and K-9 handler for the Evansville Fire Department in Evansville, Ind., and his accelerant-detector dog, Sadie, arrived at the scene, Storey was particularly interested in the home-owner. It's a known fact that arsonists enjoy watching their work, and the homeowner was particularly suspect because she was fully dressed (with socks and shoes), standing in the street, watching the fire.

Considering the speed with which the fire would have moved, there was no chance the homeowner could have gotten her shoes and socks on, Storey noted. So, he got Sadie out of the truck and walked over to the woman. "Most people aren't afraid of Sadie, and they usually ask if they can pet her," Storey says. The home-owner was no different and was delighted to see the happy black Lab. When she went to pet Sadie, Storey gave Sadie the seek command. "Sadie smelled the woman's hands, then her shoes—then she sat down rock solid," Storey chuckles. The woman's shoes were immediately bagged to be tested for accelerants the following day; the laboratory confirmed gasoline on the woman's shoes.

When the fire was finally out, Storey and Sadie returned to the scene. Sadie alerted to the site of the source of the fire and samples were taken. Again, the laboratory confirmed that gasoline was present. The woman was charged and not only served time for arson, but also on two counts of theft. And Sadie? She got some food and lots of praise for her finds, but she is probably oblivious to the fact that she serves such an important function on a daily basis.

ers, produced a number of dual champions. Not the least of Countess Howe's great Labradors was the first dual champion of the breed, Dual Ch. Banchory Bolo, the son of her very first Labrador, Scandal. It was Bolo with whom Countess Howe was most enamored, the dog who made her truly "head over hocks" for the Labrador Retriever breed.

England's royal family has long been associated with the Labrador. King George VI and Queen Elizabeth promoted Labradors at shows through their kennel known as Wolverton (more recently changed to Sandringham). The king entered dogs in the Crufts show, the U.K.'s largest dog show, in the 1920s and 1930s. The queen actually entered field trials with her dogs—this illustrates the kinds of people attracted to field trials in England! King George was the Patron of the Labrador Club, and was

Did You Know?

In 2005, *Marley & Me* shot to the top of *The New York Times* best-seller list. The book, an autobiographical account of journalist John Grogan and his Labrador Retriever, Marley, was made into a film by the same name in 2008.

replaced by Queen Elizabeth as Patroness after his death. Today in England, field trials are still supported by the royal family, and the annual championship is held at the queen's shooting estate, Sandringham, in East Anglia. She is often in attendance at the British Retriever Championship in December each year.

The British shooting dogs, or working gundogs, are athletic in type and appearance. In order for a dog to excel in a field trial, he must possess discipline, control, and responsiveness. It is much more difficult for a dog to achieve a field trial championship in Britain than it is in the United States, where field trials are simulations of hunting situations. In the United Kingdom, where the shooting sport originated, a field trial is an actual hunting episode, including wild birds and whatever else Mother Nature supplies. What makes hunting exciting is the surprise, and that element is essential to a field trial, as well.

NEXT STOP: UNITED STATES

America extends its gratitude to Countess Howe for exporting the first Labradors back to North America. Lest we forget, the Labrador Retriever began on Canadian shores! Sportsmen in Long Island, N.Y., were gifted by Countess Howe with the first

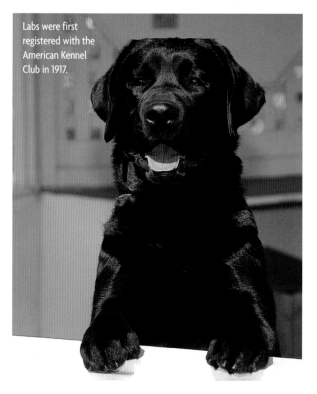

Labs were first registered with the American Kennel Club in 1917.

Labradors to be seen in the United States. This occurred shortly after World War I. Of course, the landscape of Long Island paints the perfect setting for a working Labrador, with its abundance of waterfowl, rolling oceanfront, and range of temperatures.

To say that the Labrador Retriever caught on immediately would not be true. Although the breed was first registered with the AKC in 1917, ten years later there were scarcely two dozen retrievers (of all types!) in the United States. In fact, Labradors were classified under the broad heading of "Retrievers" until the late 1920s when distinctions were made between the different breeds. The first Lab registered was a female of Scottish origin by the name of Brocklehirst Floss. The breed was officially recognized in 1932.

While today Labs are kept by all types of American families, this was not originally the case. Instead, upper-class, wealthy families were attracted to shooting sports, popular in Scotland in the 1920s. These families brought gamekeepers from Scotland onto their estates and imported Labrador

These dogs originally worked hard hauling sleds to get wood, hauling in fishing nets and picking up fish that got out of the nets. They lived on very little food. They are genetically programmed that way, and this is why they get fat so easily.—Marianne Foote of Livermore, Calif., *a Labrador Retriever breeder and Labrador Retriever Club member*

Modern-day Labs are loved as family pets, and not so much as water retrievers.

Retrievers from the finest English kennels, virtually converting their estates into shooting preserves, chock full of ducks and pheasants. It's important to note that these Labradors were imported for one purpose only—not to become beloved family pets or show dogs, but "to retrieve upland game and waterfowl." These same gentlefolk are responsible for the rise of field trials in America and thus the birth of the Labrador Retriever Club in 1931 in New York.

Franklin B. Lord, one of the club's founding members, held the club's first field trial in December 1931. A total of 27 dogs competed under two judges on an 8,000-acre estate. The club's first specialty show occurred some eighteen months later in

1933, attracting thirty-three dogs. The winner of the first specialty show was owned by Lord, a dog by the name of Boli of Blake, bred by Countess Howe. Boli also became the first bench champion of the breed.

Despite the interest in the breed that occurred between World War I and World War II, both wars had a deleterious effect on the Labrador and his numbers; this was the case with most dog breeds. It wasn't until after World War II that the Labrador Retriever gained a strong foothold in the United States. Imports from top British kennels, notably Sandylands, re-energized the breed in the United States, and these imported dogs had much influence on American conformation lines. Top British dogs and their descendants also appear in the pedigrees of many American field lines.

The trend toward two types of Labrador, those for show and those for the field, is not seen as beneficial to the breed by the national parent club. The Labrador Retriever Club feels that all Labradors should be of the same type and should be able to perform the breed's intended functions, whether or not they are destined for the field, and that this should be the first criteria when judging Labs in the show ring. It does no service to the breed to have conformation winners that are not true Labradors with working type and ability! Therefore, the club defends the standard of the breed and sets the trend for the "correct" Labrador in the United States.

The Labrador Retriever, in all colors, shapes, and sizes, reigns as America's most-registered dog. It outregisters every other breed annually and has been on the top of the list for more than a decade! As a family pet, it is the dog of choice. Whether or not the 100,000-plus Labradors registered every year with the AKC can hunt, swim, retrieve, and endure a day in the field seems immaterial to the millions of lovers of the pet Labrador. The breed's temperament and reliability, two qualities sought out by early breeders, make the Lab a flawless companion for dog folk of all ages.

Each year, the Lab is the top breed in the United States.

it's a Fact

Through much of the Lab's history, black was the color of choice. The first dogs arriving in England at Poole Harbor were black, according to record, although some sources claim chocolate dogs did exist in Newfoundland before this point. Not until the 1900s did breeders in England specifically try to improve the yellow Labs, bringing them up to the standard of the blacks. As more people met the yellow Lab, the more popular this sunny color choice became. Even though the chocolate color existed before the yellow, it has always been the least popular.

CHAPTER 3

WHERE TO LOOK

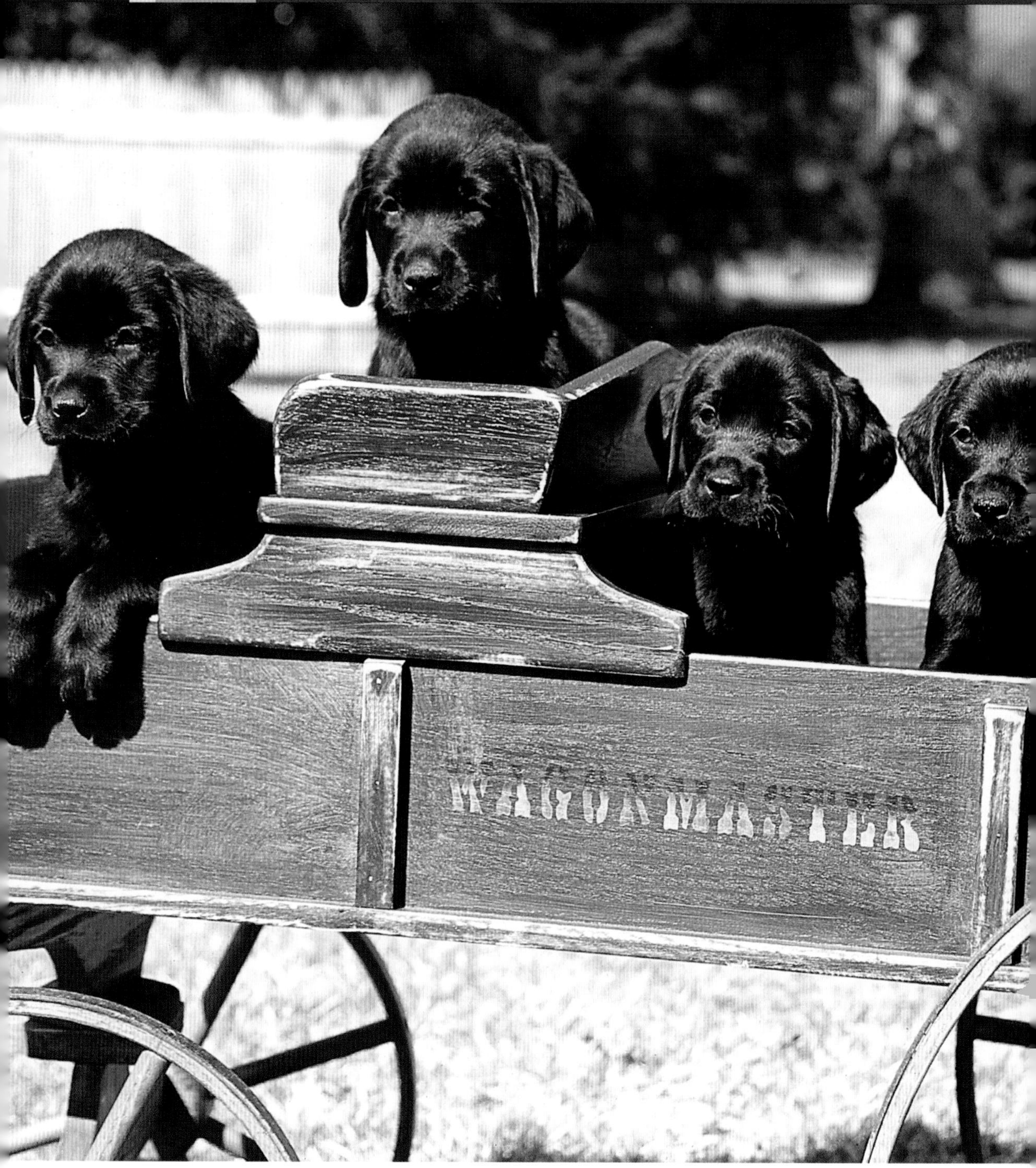

FOR A LAB

A purebred dog as versatile and talented as the Labrador Retriever attracts many admirers. Whether you are seeking a puppy simply as a home companion and family pet, as a show dog, as a field dog, or as a competition dog, there are many serious factors governing your choice. Will you have enough time to devote to your new Labrador? Even a pet Lab will require considerable time to train. Naturally, a field dog or obedience/agility dog will require hours of daily attention and special training. Do not take the acquisition of a Labrador Retriever lightly. This is a demanding dog that will want to share his whole life with you. The Labrador Retriever usually lives ten to fourteen years. Do you know where you will be in a decade? You have to plan for your Labrador Retriever to be a part of that picture.

A dog as active as the Labrador will require a lot of exercise. You must have a fenced yard, so there is no worry that your curious pup will go wandering down the lane to find your neighbors and their dogs, cats, and horses! If you are not committed to the welfare and whole existence of this energetic, purposeful animal; if, in the simplest, most basic

it's a Fact

The optimal weight of a healthy, adult Lab, according to the breed standard, is sixty-five to eighty pounds for a male and fifty-five to seventy pounds for a female.

Labs are generally happy dogs, and come in three colors: yellow, chocolate, or black.

example, you are not willing to walk your dog daily, despite the weather or how tired you are, do not choose a Labrador Retriever as a companion.

Space is another important consideration. As a puppy, a Labrador Retriever may be well accommodated in a corner of your kitchen but, after just six months, your dog will likely be more than sixty pounds, and will need more space. You will have to train your Labrador to understand the house rules so that you can trust him in every room of your house. Of course, puppyproofing is vital.

Along with exercise and space, a smart owner will need to consider the usual problems associated with puppies of any breed, such as the damages likely to be sustained by your floors, furniture, flowers, and, not least of all, restrictions to your freedom (of movement), as in vacations or

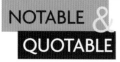

NOTABLE & QUOTABLE

Just as in the human population, personalities differ among individuals and not along color lines. A Lab is a Lab no matter what color he is.

— *Robin Anderson, a Labrador Retriever breeder in Seekonk, Mass.*

weekend trips. This union is a serious affair and should not be rushed into, but, once decided, a Labrador Retriever is, perhaps, the most rewarding of all dog breeds. A few suggestions will help in the purchase of your Lab.

ACQUIRING A PUPPY

The best place to obtain your puppy is from a reputable breeder. This is suggested even if you are not looking for a show specimen or a top contender in field work. Novice breeders and pet owners who advertise puppies at attractive prices in local newspapers are probably kind enough toward their dogs, but likely lack the expertise or facilities required to successfully raise these animals. A lack of proper feeding can cause indigestion, rickets, weak bones, poor teeth, and other problems. Veterinary bills may soon distort initial savings into financial loss, or worse, emotional loss.

Did You Know?

Signs of a Good Breeder
When you visit a breeder, be on the lookout for:
- a clean, well-maintained facility
- no overwhelming odors
- overall impression of cleanliness
- socialized dogs and puppies

Inquire about vaccinations and when the puppy was last dewormed. Check the ears. Ear-mite infestation is very common in young puppies. Left untreated, mite infestation can damage a pup's hearing. Keep on guard for the pup's scratching or shaking his head.

Color is a matter of personal choice, but whichever color you prefer, your puppy should have good pigmentation. In black Labradors, everything is black; in chocolates, the dog's nose and paws should match his color. Yellow Labs have black noses. The shades of yellows and chocolates can vary considerably, but avoid white markings, tan marks on chocolates and patches of brindle (combination of brown and black hairs). While no importance is placed on color in the breed, only the three colors—yellow, black, and chocolate—are recognized as true Labrador Retrievers.

Note the way your puppy of choice moves. The Labrador Retriever, even in puppyhood, should show light and swift movement with no tendency to stumble or drag the hind feet. Look at the mouth to make sure that the bite is fairly even, although maturity can often correct errors present at puppyhood. If you have any doubts, ask to see the parents' mouths. This brings up an important point. Do not purchase a puppy without first seeing at least one of the parents.

Be sure
you're ready
for a puppy
before you
bring one
home. Pick
up all small
things that
the pup can
get to.

Male dogs of this breed are equally devoted and loyal but have the drawback of being in season all year and, therefore, prone to possible wandering. This is the central reason why females are always chosen as guide dogs for the blind. Of course, good breeders will require that pet puppies be neutered or spayed, thus eliminating problems related to sexual behavior.

COMMITMENT OF OWNERSHIP

After considering all of these factors, you have most likely already made some very important decisions about selecting your puppy. You have chosen a Labrador Retriever, which means that you have decided which characteristics you want in a dog and what

SMART TIP!

Don't be in a hurry to take a new Lab puppy home.
The best age for Lab puppies to embark on their new lives is about at eight weeks.

type of dog will best fit into your family and lifestyle. If you have selected a breeder, you have gone a step further—you have done your research and found a responsible, conscientious person who breeds quality Labs and who should be a reliable source of help as you and your puppy adjust to life together. If you have observed a litter in action, you have obtained a firsthand look at the dynamics of a puppy pack and, thus, you have learned about each pup's individual personality—perhaps you have even found one that particularly appeals to you.

However, even if you have not yet found the Labrador Retriever of your dreams, observing pups will help you recognize certain behaviors and determine what a pup's behaviors indicate about his temperament. You will be able to pick out which pups are the leaders, which ones are less outgoing, which ones are confident, which ones are shy, playful, friendly, aggressive, etc. Equally important, you will learn to recognize what a healthy pup looks and acts like. All of these things will help you in your search, and when you find the Lab that was meant for you, you will know it.

Researching your breed, selecting a responsible breeder, and observing as many pups as possible are all important steps on the way to dog ownership. It may seem like a lot of effort; and you have not even brought the pup home yet! Remember, though, you cannot be too careful when it comes to deciding on the type of dog you want and finding out about your prospective pup's background. Buying a puppy is not—or should not be—a whimsical purchase. In fact, this is one instance in which you actually do get to choose your own family! You may be thinking that buying a puppy should be fun—it should not be so serious and so much

Q&A for Owners
Be prepared for the breeder to ask you some questions.

breeder is trying to see if you have enough time to spend each day with your new best friend, because there aren't many things sadder than a lonely Lab.

1. Have you previously owned a Labrador Retriever?
The breeder is trying to gauge how familiar you are with the breed. If you have never owned one, illustrate your knowledge of Labs by telling the breeder about your research.

2. How many hours are you away from home during the week?
Labrador Retrievers need lots of attention. They are not dogs that can just live in the backyard by themselves. The

3. How long have you wanted a Labrador Retriever?
This helps a breeder know if this purchase is an impulse buy, or a carefully thought-out decision. Buying on impulse is one of the biggest mistakes owners can make. Be patient. It may take a week to find the right dog, or even a year.

Join Club Lab to get a complete list of questions a breeder should ask you. Click on "downloads" at **DogChannel.com/Club-Lab**

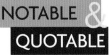
Temperaments can vary according to the aims and knowledge of the breeder. Stock selected for high performance requirements can have more exercise and training demands and may not be suitable for a less structured environment where the family is gone all day. Conversely, a low-activity, low-demand puppy may prove frustrating for the family with competition aspirations.

— breeder Marianne Foote of Livermore, Calif.

With the popularity of Labs, shelters and rescue groups across the country are often inundated with sweet, loving examples of the breed—

from the tiniest puppies to majestic senior dogs, petite females to blocky males, yellow to black to chocolate. Often, to get the Lab of your dreams, it takes just a journey to the local shelter. Or perhaps you could find your ideal dog waiting patiently in the arms of a foster parent at a nearby rescue group. It just takes a bit of effort, patience and a willingness to find the right dog for your family, not just the cutest dog on the block.

The perks of owning a Lab are plentiful: companionship, unconditional love, loyalty, laughter, and a constant exercise pal, just to name a few. So why choose the adoption option? You literally are saving a life!

Owners of adopted dogs swear they're more grateful and loving than any dog they've owned before. It's almost as if they knew what dire fate awaited them, and they are so thankful. Labs, known for their people-pleasing personalities, seem to embody this mentality whole-heartedly when they're rescued. And they want to give something back.

Another perk: Almost all adopted dogs come fully vetted, with proper medical treatment, vaccinations, medicine, as well as being spayed or neutered. Some are even licensed and microchipped.

Don't disregard older dogs, thinking the only good pair-up is between you and a puppy. Adult Labs are more established behaviorally and with their personalities, helping to better mesh their characteristics with yours in this matchmaking game. Puppies are always high in demand, so if you open your options to include adult dogs, you'll have a better chance of adopting quickly. Plus, adult dogs are often housetrained, more calm, chew-proof, and don't need to be taken outside in the middle of the night. Five times. In the rain.

The Labrador Retriever Club offers rescue support information (http://thelabradorclub.com/rescue) or you can log onto a national pet adoption website such as Petfinder.com (www.petfinder.com). The site's searchable database enables you to find a Lab puppy in your area who needs a break in the form of a compassionate owner like you.

work. Keep in mind that your puppy is not a cuddly stuffed toy or decorative lawn ornament, but instead will become a real member of your family, you will realize that while buying a puppy is a pleasurable and exciting endeavor, it is not something to be taken lightly. Relax...the fun will start when your Lab comes home! If the breeder has young puppies, he may not allow you to visit for a few weeks to ensure their safety. Whether he has puppies when you visit or not, never go from one kennel to another without going home, showering, and changing clothes, including your shoes (or clean them thoroughly, and spray the bottoms and sides with a ten-percent bleach solution). It is extremely easy to transmit deadly infectious disease and parasites from one kennel to another, even if everything looks clean.

Meet as many of your potential puppy's relatives as possible. You should be able to meet the mother unless the puppies are very young. Don't expect her to look her best while she's nursing—puppy care is a big job for canine moms. Pay attention to her temperament. It is normal for a female dog to be protective of her babies, but she should accept your presence if her owner vouches for you. If the sire (father) is on the property, ask to meet him. He may not be present, because serious breeders often breed their bitches to stud dogs owned by other people. You should be able to see pictures of him,

Quick Breeder Q&A

Here are some questions you should ask a breeder and the preferred answers you want.

Q: What color of Labrador Retrievers do you raise?

A: There is no right or wrong answer to this question. You just want to make sure the breeder has the color of Lab you want. Chocolate, yellow, or black are the three acceptable Lab colors.

Q. How often do you have litters available?

A. The answer that you want to hear from the breeder is: "once or twice a year" or "occasionally" because a breeder who doesn't have litters all that often is probably more concerned with the quality of his puppies, rather than with producing a lot of Lab puppies solely to make money.

Q. What is the goal of your breeding program?

A. A good answer is "to improve the breed" or "to breed for temperament."

Q. What kinds of health problems have you had with your Labs?

A. Beware of a breeder who says, "none." Every breed has health issues. For Labs, common problems include chronic hip dysplasia and idiopathic epilepsy.

You can get a complete list of questions to ask a Lab breeder—and the correct answers—on Club Lab. Log onto **DogChannel.com/Club-Lab** and click on "downloads."

though. If you don't like the parents—either the body type or temperament—don't buy the puppy. Pups tend to look and act like their parents.

Take a look around. Is the environment reasonably clean? Do all the dogs appear to be healthy, with clear eyes, trimmed toenails and reasonably groomed coats? Do they have fresh water to drink and room to move and play? Are they friendly? Does the breeder know every dog by name and each puppy as an individual? If the answer to any of these questions is no, look elsewhere. If the answers are yes, though, and you feel comfortable with this breeder and like his dogs, and he feels comfortable with you, you may soon be owned by a Labrador pup.

ESSENTIAL PAPERWORK

Make sure the breeder has proper papers to go with the puppy of your choice.

CONTRACT: You should receive a copy of the purchase contract you signed when you bought your puppy. The contract should specify the purchase price, health guarantee, spay/neuter requirements by a certain age, and conditions to return the pup if you find you can't keep her for any reason.

REGISTRATION PAPERS: If the breeder said that the puppy's parents were registered with the American Kennel Club or United Kennel Club, you should receive an application form to register your puppy—or at the very least, a signed bill of sale that

> **Did You Know?**
>
> **An average Labrador Retriever litter** contains six to eight puppies. Thoughtful breeders space out their litters, so they don't always have puppies available. A six-month wait is not unusual, and some breeders have waiting lists of up to two years.

you can use to register the puppy. The bill of sale should include the puppy's breed, date of birth, sex, registered names of the parents, litter number, breeder's name, date of sale, and the seller's signature. Registration allows your Lab puppy to compete in kennel club-sanctioned events, such as agility and obedience. Registration fees support research and other activities sponsored by the organization.

PEDIGREE: The breeder should include a copy of your puppy's family tree, listing your puppy's parents, grandparents, great-grandparents, and beyond, depending on how many generations the pedigree includes. It also lists any degrees and/or titles that those

Finding a healthy puppy starts with finding a quality breeder.

relatives have earned. Look for indications that the dog's ancestors were active, successful achievers in various areas of the dog sport. The information that a pedigree provides can help you understand more about the physical conformation and/or behavioral accomplishments of your pup's family. Usually the quality of the pedigree dictates the price of the puppy, so expect to pay a higher price for a higher quality pup. Chances are that you will be rewarded by the quality of life that you and your pedigreed pup will enjoy!

HEALTH RECORDS: You should receive a copy of your puppy's health records, including his date of birth, visits to the veterinarian and immunizations. Bring the health records to your veterinarian when you take your puppy in for his first checkup, which should take place within a few days of his arrival in your household. The records will become part of your puppy's permanent health file.

CARE INSTRUCTIONS: Finally, the breeder should provide written instructions on basic puppy care, including when and how much to feed your Lab.

Signs of a Healthy Puppy

Here are a few things you should look for when selecting a puppy from a litter.

1. NOSE: It should be slightly moist to the touch, but there shouldn't be excessive discharge. The puppy should not be sneezing or sniffling persistently.

2. SKIN AND COAT: The puppy's coat should be soft and shiny, without flakes or excessive shedding. Watch out for patches of missing hair, redness, bumps, or sores. The pup should have a pleasant smell.

3. BEHAVIOR: A healthy puppy may be sleepy, but should not be lethargic. A healthy pup will be playful at times, not isolated in a corner. You should see occasional bursts of energy and interaction with littermates.

There are more signs to look for when picking out the perfect Labrador Retriever puppy for you. Download the list at **DogChannel.com/Club-Lab**

Maybe rescue is what you are searching for.

When Dianne Marcinizyn and her husband, Rob McMahon, of Scottsdale, Ariz., began looking for a dog, they immediately turned to rescue. "We have several friends who have dogs and through talking with them, learned of the over-population problem and just how many dogs are on the euthanasia list because of something as simple as a shortage of housing," Marcinizyn says.

She found Lola, a loveable Lab with a goofy grin, on the Desert Labrador Retriever Rescue website (www.dlrrphoenix.org). "It wasn't until later that we would learn that she had been living in a crate for six years, and the silly look on her face was actually fear," she says. "We were told she was a puppy mill dog and had been dumped at the pound by her breeder. After she served her purpose for profit, she was left for dead."

Lola melted their hearts from the get-go. She displayed a gentle energy and love that could only be manifested in a happily wagging tail as she ran to greet Marcinizyn. "Her belly swung from side to side and she couldn't have been more beautiful to us," she says. "We burst into tears and adopted her on the spot. Belly or no belly, she was our six-year-old baby from that moment forward."

Even though she was rescued physically, Lola's soul still needed saving. She was so shy at first, allowing hardly any physical contact. The tattoo in her ear proved she was never more than a number. Sure, Lola was happy to be home, but she seemed uncomfortable with too much love and attention.

"If we got too close for too long, she would get up and move away from us," Marcinizyn says. "All we could assume was that it was probably her first experience with human contact."

Hand-feeding, love, patience and more love helped Lola experience the beauty of family within a few weeks. Marcinizyn worked with her on walks and through training, even adopting a second Lab, two-year-old Luigi, who has helped Lola gain confidence and really blossom.

And as this pack grew, so did Marcinizyn's desire to do more. She saw first-hand the benefits of adoption, and wanted to help others experience the joy she and McMahon experienced daily with their Labs. In 2006, they became a foster family to other Labs in need.

ESSENTIALS

Researching your breed and finding a breeder are only two aspects of the homework you will have to do before bringing your Labrador Retriever puppy home. You also will have to prepare your home and family for the new addition.

Much like you would prepare a nursery for a newborn baby, you will need to designate a place in your home that will be the puppy's own. How you prepare your home will depend on how much freedom the dog will be allowed: Will he be confined to a specific area in the house, or will he be allowed to roam as he pleases? Whatever you decide, you must ensure that he has a place that he can call his own.

When you bring your new Labrador puppy into your home, you are bringing him into what will become *his* home, as well. Obviously, you did not buy a puppy so that he could take control of your house, but in order for a puppy to grow into a stable, well-adjusted dog, he has to feel comfortable in his surroundings. Remember, he is leaving

it's a Fact

Dangers lurk indoors and out. Keep your curious Labrador Retriever from investigating your shed and garage. Antifreeze and fertilizers, such as those you would use for roses, will kill a Lab. Keep these items on high shelves that are out of reach for your low-sniffing retriever.

A well-stocked toy box should contain three main categories of toys.
1. **action** (anything that you can throw or roll and get things moving)
2. **distraction** (durable toys that make dogs work for a treat)
3. **comfort** (soft, stuffed little "security blankets"

the warmth and security of his mother and littermates, plus the familiarity of the only place he has ever known, so it is important to make his transition as easy as possible. Be a smart owner and prepare a place in your home for the puppy, and make him feel as welcome as possible in a strange, new place. It should not take him long to get used to it, but the sudden shock of being transplanted is somewhat traumatic for a young Lab. Imagine how a small child would feel in the same situation—that is how your puppy must be feeling. It is up to you to reassure him and to let him know, "Little fellow, you are going to like it here!"

PUPPYPROOFING

Aside from making sure that your Labrador Retriever will be comfortable in your home, you also have to make sure that your home is safe, which means taking the proper precautions to keep your pup away from things that are dangerous for him.

Keep your Lab safe by deeming certain areas off limits, such as fireplace hearths.

Puppyproof your home inside and out. Place breakables out of reach. If he is limited to certain places within the house, keep potentially dangerous items in off-limit areas. If your Labrador Retriever is going to spend time in a crate, make sure that there is nothing near his crate that he can reach if he sticks his curious little nose or paws through the openings.

The outside of your home must also be safe for your pup. Your puppy will naturally want to run and explore the yard, and he should be granted that freedom—as long as you are there to supervise him. Do not let a fence give you a false sense of security; you would be surprised how crafty (and persist-

ent) a dog can be in figuring out how to dig under a fence or squeeze his way through holes. The remedy is to make the fence well embedded into the ground. Be sure to repair or secure any gaps in the fence. Check the fence periodically to ensure that it is in good shape and make repairs as needed; a

Did You Know? The drive to carry is in your Lab puppy's genes. Labs were bred to be hunting dogs, and he's designed— physically and mentally—to carry things back to people.

When puppy-proofing your house, be sure to check the yard for any potential dangers.

very determined pup may work on the same spot until he is able to get through.

The following are a few common problem areas to watch out for in the home.

ELECTRICAL CORDS AND WIRING: No electrical cord or wiring is safe. Office-supply stores sell products to keep wires gathered under computer desks, as well as products that prevent office chair wheels (and puppy teeth) from damaging electrical cords. If you have exposed cords and wires, these products aren't very expensive and can be used to keep a pup out of trouble.

TRASH CANS: Don't waste your time trying to train your Lab not to get into the trash. Simply put the trash or garbage behind a cabinet door and use a child-safe lock if necessary. Be aware that dogs love bathroom trash (i.e., cotton balls, cotton swabs, used razors, dental floss, etc.), which consists of items that are all extremely dangerous! Put this trash can in a cabinet under the sink and make sure you always shut the door to the bathroom.

HOUSEHOLD CLEANERS: Make sure your puppy doesn't have access to any of

JOIN OUR ONLINE **Lab Club**

Before you bring your Labrador home, make sure you don't have anything that can put him in harm's way. Go to Club Lab and download a list of poisonous plants and foods to avoid. Log on to **DogChannel.com/Club-Lab** and click on "downloads."

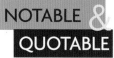

The first thing you should always do before your puppy comes home is to lie on the ground and look around. You want to be able to see everything your puppy is going to see. For the puppy, the world is one big chew toy.

—Cathleen Stamm, rescue volunteer in San Diego, Calif.

9-1-1! If you don't know whether the plant or food or "stuff" your Labrador just ate is toxic to dogs, you can call the ASPCA's Animal Poison Control Center (888-426-4435). Be prepared to provide your puppy's age and weight, his symptoms—if any—and how much of the plant, chemical, or substance the puppy ingested, as well as how long ago you think he came into contact with the substance. The ASPCA charges a consultation fee for this service.

these deadly chemicals. Keep them behind closed cabinet doors, using child-safe locks if necessary.

PEST CONTROL SPRAYS AND POISONS: Chemicals to control ants or other pests should never be used in the house, if possible. Your puppy doesn't have to directly ingest these poisons to become ill; if the Lab steps in the poison, he can experience toxic effects by licking his paws. Roach motels and other poisonous pest traps are also evidently yummy to dogs, so don't drop these poisons behind couches or cabinets.

FABRIC: Here's one you might not think about: Some puppies have a habit of licking blankets, upholstery, rugs, or carpets. Though this habit seems fairly innocuous, over time the fibers from the upholstery or carpet can accumulate in the dog's stomach and cause a blockage. If you see your dog licking any of these items, remove the item or prevent your Lab from having contact with it.

PRESCRIPTIONS, PAINKILLERS, SUPPLEMENTS AND VITAMINS: Keeping medications on a counter or the kitchen table isn't safe. All medications should be kept in a high cabinet. Also, be very careful when taking your prescription medications, supplements, or vitamins: How often have you dropped a pill? With a Labrador Retriever, you can be assured that your puppy will be in between your legs and will snarf up the pill before you can even start to say "No!" Dispense your own pills carefully and without your Lab present.

Though Labs are generally kid-friendly, owners should supervise all play between children and their Lab.

MISCELLANEOUS LOOSE ITEMS: If it's not bolted to the floor, your puppy is likely to give the item a taste test. Socks, coins, children's toys, game pieces, cat bell balls—you name it; if it's on the floor, it's worth a try. Make sure the floors in your home are picked up and free of clutter.

FAMILY INTRODUCTIONS

Everyone in the house will be excited about the puppy's homecoming and will want to pet him and play with him. It is best to make the introduction low-key so as not to overwhelm the puppy. He is apprehensive already. It is the first time he

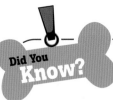

has been separated from his mother, littermates, and the breeder, and the ride to your home is likely to be the first time he has been in a car. The last thing you want to do is smother your Labrador Retriever, as this will only frighten him further. This is not to say that human contact is not extremely necessary at this stage, because this is the time when a connection between the pup and his human family is formed. Gentle petting and soothing words should help console your Labrador Retriever, as well as just putting him down and letting him explore on his own (under your watchful eye, of course).

The pup may approach the family members or busy himself with exploring for a while. Gradually, each person should spend some time with the pup, one at a time, crouching down to get as close to the Lab's level as possible and letting him sniff their hands before petting him gently. He definitely needs human attention and he needs to be touched; this is how to form an immediate bond. Just remember that the pup is experiencing a lot of things for the first time, at the same time. There are new people, new noises, new smells, and new things to investigate, so be gentle, be affectionate, and be as comforting as you can be.

PUP'S FIRST NIGHT HOME

You have traveled home with your new charge safely in his crate. He may have already been to the vet for a thorough checkup, he's been weighed, his papers examined; perhaps he's even been vaccinated and wormed as well. Your Labrador Retriever has met and licked the whole family, including the excited children and

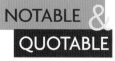

NOTABLE & QUOTABLE

Playing with toys from puppyhood encourages good behavior and social skills throughout the dog's life. A happy, playful dog is a content and well-adjusted one. Also, because all puppies chew to soothe their gums and help loosen puppy teeth, they should always have easy access to several different toys.—trainer, author and radio host Harrison Forbes of Savannah, Tenn.

the less-than-happy cat. He's explored his area, his new bed, the yard, and anywhere else he's permitted. He's eaten his first meal at home and relieved himself in the proper place. Your Labrador Retriever has heard lots of new sounds, smelled new friends, and seen more of the outside world than ever before.

This was just the first day! He's worn out and is ready for bed—or so you think! Remember, this is your puppy's first night to sleep alone. His mother and littermates are no longer at paw's length, and he's scared, cold, and lonely. Be reassuring to your new family member. This is not the time to spoil your Labrador Retriever and give in to his inevitable whining.

Puppies whine to let others know where they are and hopefully to get company out of it. Place your pup in his new bed or crate in his room and close the door. Mercifully, he may fall asleep without a peep. If, however, the inevitable occurs, ignore the whining; he is fine. Do not give in and visit the pup. He will fall asleep eventually.

Funny Bone

Q. What breed would you get if you crossed a Labrador Retriever and a Curly-Coated Retriever?
A. Lab Coat Retriever!

Many breeders recommend placing a piece of bedding from his former home in his new bed so that he recognizes the scent of his littermates. Others still advise placing a hot water bottle in his bed for warmth. The latter may be a good idea provided the pup doesn't attempt to suckle; he'll get good and wet and may not fall asleep so fast.

Your Labrador Retriever's first night can be somewhat stressful for him and his new family. Remember that you are setting the tone of nighttime at your house. Unless you want to play with your pup every night at 10 p.m., midnight, and 2 a.m., don't initiate

Your pup's first night home will be full of excitement; he probably will be worn out by the end of the day.

Supervise the use of plush toys. Noise-making squeakers, ripped cloth and stuffing can cause a dangerous bowel blockage or choke your Labrador if they are swallowed.

SMART TIP!

the habit. Your family will thank you, and so will your pup!

SHOPPING FOR A LAB

It's fun shopping for a new puppy. From training to feeding and sleeping to playing, your new Lab will need a few items to make life comfy, easy, and fun. Be prepared and visit your local pet-supply store before you bring home your new family member.

Collar and ID tag: Accustom your dog to wearing a collar the first day you bring him home. Not only will a collar and ID tag help your pup in the event that he becomes lost, but collars are also an important training tool. If your Lab gets into trouble, the collar will act as a handle, helping you divert him to a more appropriate behavior. Make sure the collar fits snugly enough so that your Lab cannot wriggle out of it, but is loose enough so that it will not be uncomfortably tight around his neck. You should be able to fit a finger between the pup and the collar. Collars come in many styles, but for starting out, a simple buckle collar with an easy-release snap works great.

Leash: For training or just for taking a stroll down the street, a leash is your Lab's

When shopping for a Lab, some essential things to purchase include a collar, ID tag, and leash.

vehicle to explore the outside world. Like collars, leashes come in a variety of styles and materials. A six-foot nylon leash is a popular choice because they are lightweight and durable. As your pup grows and gets used to walking on the leash, you may want to purchase a flexible leash. These leads allow you to extend the length to give the dog a broader area to explore or to shorten the length to keep the dog closer to you. Of course there are special leashes for training purposes, and specially made harnesses for working dogs, but these are not necessary for routine walks.

Bowls: Your Labrador Retriever will need two bowls: one for water and one for food. You may want two sets of bowls, one for inside and one for outside, depending on where the dog will be fed and where he will be spending time. Bowls should be sturdy enough so that they don't tip over easily. (Most have reinforced bottoms that prevent tipping.) Bowls should be made from metal, ceramic, or plastic, and each should be easy to clean.

It is advisable to put your Lab's food and water bowls on elevated bowl stands; this brings the bowls closer to the dog's level so he does not have to crane his neck to eat or drink, thus aiding his digestion and helping to guard against bloat or gastric torsion, a condition that affects deep-chested dogs like the Labrador.

Crate: A crate is multipurpose. It serves as a bed, house-training tool, and travel carrier. It also is the ideal doggie den—a bedroom of sorts—that your Labrador Retriever can retire to when he wants to rest or just needs a break. The crate should be large enough for your Labrador Retriever to stand in, turn around and lie down. You don't want any more room than this—especially if you're planning on using the crate to house-train your dog—because he will eliminate in one corner and lie down in another. Get a crate that is big enough for your dog when he is an adult. Then use dividers to limit the space when he's a puppy.

Bed: A plush bed will make sleeping and resting more comfortable for your Lab. Dog beds come in all shapes, sizes, and colors, but your dog just needs one that is soft and large enough for him to stretch out on. Because puppies and rescue dogs often don't come house-trained, it's helpful to buy a bed that can be washed easily. If your Lab will be sleeping in a crate, a crate pad and a small blanket that he can "burrow" in will help him feel more at home. Replace the blanket if it becomes ragged and starts to fall apart because your Lab's nails could get caught in it.

Gate: Similar to those used for toddlers, gates help keep your Labrador Retriever confined to one room or area when you can't supervise him. Gates also work to keep your dog out of areas you don't want him in.

Gates are available in many styles. For Labs, make sure the one you choose has openings small enough so your dog can't squeeze through the bars or openings on the gate.

Toys: Keep your Labrador Retriever occupied and entertained by providing him with an array of fun toys. Teething puppies like to chew—in fact, chewing is a physical need for pups as they are teething—and everything from your shoes to the leather couch to the Oriental rug is fair game. Divert your Lab's chewing instincts with durable toys like bones made of nylon or hard rubber. Other fun toys include rope toys, treat-dispensing toys, and balls. Make sure the toys and bones don't have any small parts that could break off and be swallowed, causing your dog to choke. Stuffed toys are popular, but they can become destuffed, and an overly excited puppy may ingest the stuffing or the squeaker. Check your Lab's toys regularly and replace them if they become frayed or show signs of wear.

Every puppy (but especially Labs!) needs plenty of toys, so be sure to stock up on lots of different kinds.

Cleaning supplies: Until your pup is house-trained, you will be cleaning up a lot of accidents, which is acceptable in the beginning because your Labrador Retriever puppy will not know any better. All you can do is be prepared to clean up any accidents. Old rags, towels, newspapers, and a stain and odor remover are certainly good to have on hand.

BEYOND THE BASICS

The items previously discussed are the bare necessities. You will find out what else you need as you go along—grooming supplies, flea/tick protection, etc. These things will vary depending on your situation, but it is important that you have everything you need to feed and make your Labrador Retriever comfortable during his first few days at home.

Some ordinary household items make great toys for your Labrador—as long you make sure they are safe.
You will find a list of homemade toys at **DogChannel.com/Club-Lab**

HOUSE-TRAINING

One of the high-priority goals for smart Labrador owners is house-training, which is teaching your pup when and where to go to the bathroom. In theory, house-training is simple: Manage your pup so he doesn't have the chance to make mistakes, and give him tons of reinforcement for going where you want him to. That's a simple theory, perhaps, but not always so in practice.

The good news about the frequency of puppy elimination is that it gives you lots of opportunities to help your pup learn how to go in the right spot. The bad news is that it means you have to constantly supervise him; you'll be amazed by how quickly he can squat and pee the instant you're not watching.

In any case, successful house-training takes supervision and good management—crates, tethers, exercise pens, and leashes—until you know your dog has developed substrate preferences for outside surfaces (grass, gravel, concrete), instead of carpet, tile, or hardwood, and knows that potty happens outside.

it's a Fact

Ongoing house-training difficulties may indicate your puppy has a health problem, warranting a veterinary checkup. A urinary infection, parasites, a virus, and other nasty issues greatly affect your puppy's ability to hold pee or poop.

IN THE BEGINNING

For the first two to three weeks of a puppy's life, his mother helps him eliminate. The mother also keeps the whelping box or "nest area" clean. When pups begin to walk around and eat on their own, they choose for themselves where they eliminate.

You can train your puppy to relieve himself wherever you choose, but this must be somewhere suitable. You should bear in mind from the outset that when your puppy is old enough to go out in public places, any canine deposits must be removed at once. You will always have to carry a small plastic bag or "poop-scoop" with you.

Outdoor training includes such surfaces as grass, soil, and concrete. Indoor training usually means training your dog on newspaper. When deciding on the surface and location that you will want your Labrador Retriever to use, be sure it is going to be permanent. Training your dog to eliminate on grass and then changing your mind two months later is extremely difficult for dog and owner.

Next, choose the cue you will use each and every time you want your pup to void. "Let's go," "hurry up," and "potty" are examples of cues commonly used by owners. Get in the habit of giving the puppy your

Did You Know?

Cleaning accidents properly with an enzyme solution will dramatically reduce the time it takes to house-train your dog because he won't be drawn back to the same areas.

chosen relief command before you take him out. That way, when he becomes an adult, you will be able to determine if he wants to go out when you ask him. A confirmation will be signs of interest, such as wagging his tail, watching you intently, or going to the door.

LET'S START WITH THE CRATE

Clean animals by nature, dogs keenly dislike soiling where they sleep and eat. This fact makes a crate a useful tool for housetraining. When purchasing a new crate, consider that one correctly sized will allow adequate room for an adult dog to stand full-height, lie on his side without scrunching, and turn around easily.

Some crates come equipped with a movable wall that reduces the interior size to provide enough space for your puppy to stand, turn, and lie down, while not allowing room to soil one end and sleep in the other. The problem is that if your puppy goes potty in the crate anyway, the divider forces him to lie in his own excrement. This can work against you by desensitizing your puppy against his normal, instinctive revulsion to resting where he's eliminated.

If scheduling permits you or a responsible family member to clean the crate soon after it's soiled, feel free to use this aid, as limiting crate size does encourage your puppy to hold it. Otherwise, give your Labrador Retriever enough room to move

Just because your puppy sleeps for six or more hours through the night, does not mean he can hold it that long during the more active daytime hours.

away from an unclean area until he's better able to control his elimination.

One last bit of advice on the crate: Place it in the corner of a normally trafficked room, such as the family room or kitchen. Social and curious by nature, Labs like to feel included in family happenings. Creating a quiet retreat by putting the crate in an unused area may seem like a good idea, but results in your puppy feeling insecure and isolated. Watching his people pop in and out of the crate room reassures your puppy that he's not forgotten.

Needless to say, not every puppy adheres to this guideline. If your puppy moves along at a faster pace, thank your lucky stars. Should he progress slower, accept it, and remind yourself that he'll improve. Be aware that pups frequently hold it longer at night than during the day.

Take your pup to the same spot to potty to get him in the habit of knowing where to "go."

True Tails

Laurie Breisch recalls one memorable Christmas, when she was dog sitting her son's Lab, Bear, but was untested in the face of Lab food-acquiring ingenuity.

"I was upstairs changing my clothes when I heard a 'thunk,'" she says. "Something food-related had hit the floor. I raced downstairs and found the one and only green vegetable dish I had prepared flipped over on the floor. It was a new recipe I had learned in my Italian cooking class, and I was excited to be serving this special dish on Christmas Day.

"The pan was upside down, and my only thought was getting it off the floor and removing all the dog hair so no one would be the wiser! But when I picked up the pan, it was empty. Bear had consumed 30 zucchini rolls in marinara sauce, toothpicks and all," Breisch recalls.

After consulting with two emergency clinics wise in the ways of Labrador dining habits, Laurie let nature take it course, and the toothpicks exited Bear in a natural way.

On another occasion, Bear consumed two bars of soap, still in their boxes. Being well house-trained, he would go out, vomit and return to drink water, which resulted in decorative bubbles around his mouth.

PUPPY'S NEEDS

Your Labrador Retriever needs to relieve himself after play periods, after each meal, after he has been sleeping, and any time he indicates that he is looking for a place to urinate or defecate.

The urinary and intestinal tract muscles of very young puppies are not fully developed. Therefore, like human babies, puppies need to relieve themselves frequently. Take your puppy out often—every hour for an eight-week-old, for example—and always immediately after sleeping and eating. The older the puppy, the less often he will need to relieve

himself. Finally, as a mature healthy adult, he will require only three to five relief trips per day.

HOUSING HELP

Because the types of housing and control you provide for your puppy have a direct relationship on the success of house-training, consider the various aspects of both before beginning training.

Taking a new puppy home and turning him loose in your house can be compared to turning a child loose in a sports arena and telling the child that the place is all his! The

How often does a Lab puppy do his business? A lot! Go to **DogChannel.com/Club-Lab** and download the typical peeing and pooping schedule of a puppy. You can also download a chart that you can fill out to track your dog's elimination timetable, which will help you with house-training.

JOIN OUR
ONLINE
Lab
Club

sheer enormity of the place would be too much for him to handle.

Instead, offer your puppy clearly defined areas where he can play, sleep, eat, and live. A room of the house where the family gathers is the most obvious choice. Puppies are social animals and need to feel a part of the pack right from the start. Hearing your voice, watching you while you are doing things, and smelling you nearby are all positive reinforcers that he is now a member of your pack. Usually a family room, the kitchen or a nearby adjoining breakfast area is ideal for providing safety and security for both puppy and owner.

Within that room, there should be a smaller area that the puppy can call his own. An alcove, a wire or fiberglass dog crate, or a fenced (not boarded!) corner from which he can view the activities of his new family will be fine. The size of the area or crate is the key factor here. The area must be large enough for the puppy to lie down and stretch out his little body, yet small enough so that he cannot relieve himself at one end and sleep at the other without coming into contact with his droppings before he is fully trained to relieve himself outside.

The designated area should be lined with clean bedding and a toy that your puppy enjoys. Water must always be available, in a nonspill bowl, once your Labrador puppy is housebroken reliably.

House-training your pup takes lots of patience and practice.

IN CONTROL

By control, we mean helping your pup create a lifestyle pattern that will be compatible to that of his human pack (you!). Just as we guide youngsters to learn our

way of life, we must show our puppy when it is time to play, eat, sleep, exercise, and entertain himself.

Your puppy should always sleep in his crate. He should also learn that, during times of household confusion and excessive human activity, such as at breakfast when family members are preparing for the day, he can play by himself in relative safety and comfort in his designated area. Each time you leave the puppy alone, he should understand exactly where he is to stay. Puppies are chewers. They cannot tell the difference between lamp cords, television wires, shoes, or table legs. Dangerous situations may arise.

Reward your pup with a high-value treat immediately after he potties to reinforce going in the proper location, then play for a short time afterward. This teaches that good things happen after pottying outside!—Victoria Schade, certified pet dog trainer, from Annandale, Va.

Potty time isn't play time, despite what your pup might think! Make sure he stays on task.

Chewing into a television wire, for example, can be fatal to the puppy, while a shorted wire can start a fire in the house.

If the puppy chews on the arm of the chair when he is alone, you will probably discipline him angrily when you get home. Thus, he makes the association that your coming home means he is going to be punished. (He will not remember chewing the chair and is incapable of making the association of the discipline with his naughty deed.)

Other times of excitement, such as family parties, can be fun for your Labrador puppy, providing that he can view the activities from the security of his designated area. He is not underfoot, and he is not being fed all sorts of tidbits that will probably cause him stomach distress, yet he still feels a part of the fun.

Did You Know?

White vinegar is a good odor remover if you don't have aprofessional cleaner on hand; use one quarter cup to one quart of water.

SCHEDULE

Your Labrador Retriever puppy should be taken to his relief area each time he is released from his designated area, after meals, after play sessions, and when he first awakens in the morning (at age eight weeks, this can mean before sunrise!). The puppy will indicate that he's ready to go by circling or sniffing busily; do not misinterpret these signs. For a puppy younger than ten weeks of age, a routine of taking him out every hour is necessary. As the puppy grows, he will be able to wait for longer periods of time.

Keep trips to his relief area short. Stay no more than five or six minutes and then return to the house. If your Lab goes during that time, praise him lavishly and take him indoors immediately. If he does not, but he has an accident when you go back indoors, pick him up immediately, say "No! No!" and return to his relief area. Wait a few minutes, then return to the house again. Never hit a puppy or rub his face in urine or excrement when he has had an accident.

Once indoors, put the puppy in his crate

until you have had time to clean up his accident. Then release him to the family area and watch him more closely than before. Chances are, your Lab's accident was a result of your not picking up on his signal or waiting too long before offering him the opportunity to relieve himself. Never hold a grudge against the puppy for accidents.

Let the puppy learn that going outdoors means it is time to relieve himself, not to play. Once trained, he will be able to play indoors and out and still differentiate between the times for play versus the times for relief.

Help him develop regular hours for naps, being alone, playing by himself, and just resting, all in his crate. Encourage your Lab to entertain himself while you are busy with your activities. Let him learn that having you nearby is comforting, but it is not your main purpose in life to provide him with undivided attention.

Each time you put a puppy in his own area, use the same command, whatever suits you best. Soon he will run to his crate or special area when he hears you say those words.

Crate-training provides safety for you, the puppy and the home. It also provides your Labrador with a feeling of security, and that helps the puppy achieve self-confidence and clean habits.

Remember that one of the primary ingredients in house-training your puppy is control. Regardless of your lifestyle, there will always be occasions when you will need to have a place where your Labrador can stay and be happy and safe. Crate-training is the answer for now and in the future.

A few key elements are really all you need for a successful house-training method—consistency, frequency, praise, control, and supervision. By following these procedures with a normal, healthy puppy, you and your Labrador Retriever puppy will soon be past the stage of "accidents" and ready to move on to a full and rewarding life together.

Having house-training problems with your Labrador Retriever? Ask other Lab owners for advice and tips. Log onto **DogChannel.com/Club-Lab** and click on "community."

VET VISITS AND

EVERYDAY CARE

Selecting a veterinarian should be based on his skills with dogs, and, if possible, experience with Labrador Retrievers. It will be helpful if the vet is based nearby, too, because you might have an emergency or need to make multiple visits for treatments.

FIRST STEP: SELECT THE RIGHT VET

All licensed veterinarians are capable of dealing with routine medical issues such as infections and injuries, as well as the promotion of health (for example, by vaccinations). If the problem affecting your dog is more complex, your veterinarian will refer you to someone with a more detailed knowledge of what is wrong. This will usually be a specialist who is a veterinary dermatologist, veterinary ophthalmologist, etc., whatever field you require.

Veterinary procedures are very costly and, as the treatments available improve, they are going to become more expensive. It is quite acceptable to discuss matters of cost with your vet; if there is more than one treatment option, cost may be a factor in deciding which route to take.

Smart owner's look for a veterinarian before they actually need one. For newbie pet owners, ideally start looking for a veterinarian a month or two before you bring home your new Lab puppy. That will give you time to meet candidate veterinarians, check out the condition of the clinic, and see who you feel comfortable with. If you already have a pet, look sooner rather than later, preferably not in the midst of a veterinary health crisis.

Second, define the criteria that are important to you. Points to consider or investigate:

Convenience: Proximity to your home, extended hours, or drop-off services are helpful for people who work regular business hours, have a busy schedule, or don't want to drive far. If you have mobility issues, finding a veterinarian who makes house calls or a service that provides pet transport might be particularly important.

Size: A one-person practice ensures that you'll always be dealing with the same veterinarian during each and every visit. "That person can really get to know you and your dog," says Bernadine Cruz, D.V.M., of Laguna Hills Animal Hospital in California. The downside, though, is the sole practitioner does not have the immediate input of another veterinarian, and if your vet becomes ill or takes time off, you are out of luck.

The multiple-doctor practice offers consistency if your pet needs to come in unexpectedly on a day when your veterinarian isn't there. Additionally, vet can quickly consult with their colleagues within the clinic if they're unsure about a diagnosis or treatment.

If you find a veterinarian within that practice who you really like, you can make your appointments with that individual, establishing the same kind of bond that you would with the solo practitioner.

Appointment Policies: Some practices are strictly by-appointment only, which could minimize your wait time. However, if a sudden problem arises with your Lab and the veterinarians are booked up, they might not be able to squeeze your pet in that day. Some clinics are drop-in only —great for impromptu or crisis visits, but without scheduling may involve longer waits to see the next available veterinarian—whoever is open, not someone in particular. Some practices maintain an appointment schedule but also keep slots open throughout the day for walk-ins, offering the best of both worlds.

Basic vs. State-of-the-Art vs. Full Service: A practice with high-tech equipment offers greater diagnostic capabilities and treatment options, important for tricky or difficult cases. However, the cost of pricey equipment is passed along to the client, so you

Keep your Lab at the peak of health by visiting the vet for regular checkups.

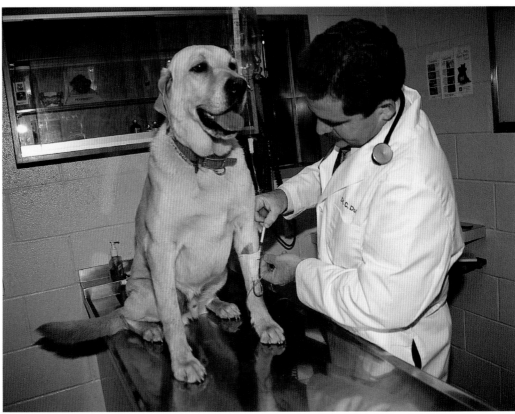

The vet will be an important part of your dog's life, so be sure you and your Lab are comfortable with him.

could pay more for routine procedures—the bulk of most pets' appointments. Some practices offer boarding, grooming, training classes, and other services on the premises, a convenience some pet owners appreciate.

Fees and Payment Polices: How much is a routine office call? If there is a significant price difference, ask why. If you intend to carry health insurance on your Lab or want to pay by credit card, make sure the candidate clinic accepts those payment options.

FIRST VET VISIT

It is much easier, less costly, and more effective to practice preventative medicine than to fight bouts of illness and disease. Properly bred puppies of all breeds come from parents who were selected based upon their genetic disease profile. The puppies' mother should have been vaccinated, free of all internal and external parasites, and properly nourished. For these reasons, a visit to the veterinarian who

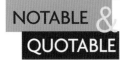

NOTABLE & QUOTABLE

Tricuspid valve dysplasia is a malformation of the heart valve that separates two chambers of the right side of the heart. The malformation reduces the heart's efficiency in pumping blood to the lungs, resulting in backflow and abnormal pressure in the heart. Eventually, congestive heart failure occurs.—Marcia King, medical writer from Toledo, Ohio

cared for the dam (mother) is recommended if at all possible. The dam passes disease resistance to her puppies, which should last from eight to ten weeks. Unfortunately, she can also pass on parasites and infection. This is why knowledge about her health is useful in learning more about the health of the puppies.

Now that you have your Labrador Retriever puppy home safe and sound, it's time to arrange your pup's first trip to the veterinarian. Perhaps the breeder can recommend someone in the area who specializes in Labrador Retrievers, or maybe you know some other Lab owners who can suggest a good vet. Either way, you should make an appointment within a couple of days of bringing home your puppy. If possible, see if you can stop for this first vet appointment before going home.

The pup's first vet visit will consist of an overall examination to make sure that the pup does not have any problems that are not apparent to you. The veterinarian also will set up a schedule for the pup's vaccinations; the breeder will inform you of which ones the dog has already received, and the vet can continue from there.

The puppy also will have his teeth examined and have his skeletal conformation and general health checked prior to certification by the veterinarian. Puppies in certain breeds have problems with their kneecaps, cataracts and other eye problems, heart murmurs, and undescended

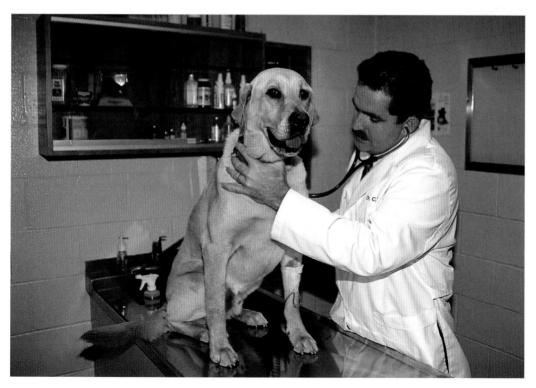

testicles. They may also have personality problems, and your veterinarian might have training in temperament evaluation.

VACCINATION SCHEDULING

Most vaccinations are given by injection and should only be given by a veterinarian. Both you and the vet should keep a record of the date of the injection, the identification of the vaccine, and the amount given. Some vets give a first vaccination at eight weeks of age, but most dog breeders prefer the course not to commence until about ten weeks because of interaction with the antibodies produced by the mother. The vaccination scheduling is usually based on a fifteen-day cycle. You must take your vet's advice as to when to vaccinate, as this may differ according to the vaccine used.

The usual vaccines contain immunizing doses of several different viruses such as distemper, parvovirus, parainfluenza, and hepatitis. There are other vaccines available when the puppy is at risk. You should rely upon professional advice. This is especially true for the booster immunizations. Most vaccination programs require a booster when the puppy is a year old and once a year thereafter. In some cases, circumstances may require more frequent immunizations.

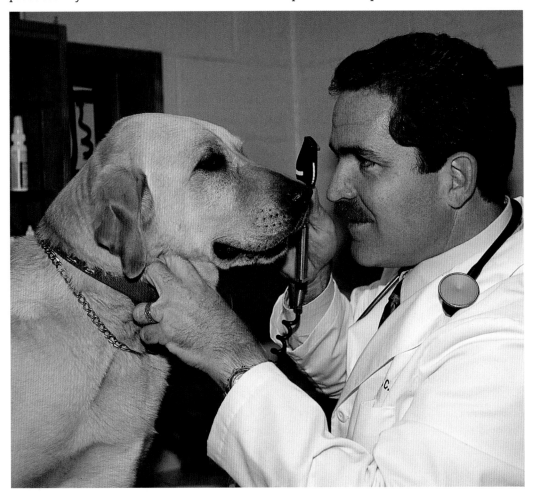

Large-breed dogs are more susceptible to chronic hip dysplasia and, unfortunately, Labs see their share of the disease. According to the Orthopedic Foundation for Animals, 13.2 percent of Lab radiographs presented to the OFA were dysplastic. The true incidence of CHD is probably higher, because many dysplastic dogs' films are never sent to OFA.

—Marcia King, medical writer from Toledo, Ohio

When searching for a vet, ask dog-lovers in your area for advice.

Canine cough, more formally known as tracheobronchitis, is immunized against with a vaccine that is sprayed into the dog's nostrils. Canine cough is usually included in routine vaccination, but it is often not as effective as the vaccines for other major diseases.

Your veterinarian will probably recommend that your Labrador Retriever puppy be fully vaccinated before you bring him outside. There are airborne diseases, parasite eggs in the grass, and unexpected visits from other dogs that might be dangerous to your puppy's health. Other dogs are the most harmful reservoir of pathogenic organisms, as everything they have can be transmitted to your puppy.

Five Months to One Year of Age: Unless you intend to breed or show your dog, neutering the puppy at six months of age is recommended. Discuss this with your veterinarian. Neutering/spaying has proven to be beneficial to male and female puppies,

respectively. Besides eliminating the possibility of pregnancy, it inhibits (but does not prevent) breast cancer in females and prostate cancer in male dogs.

Your veterinarian should provide your Labrador puppy with a thorough dental evaluation at six months of age, ascertaining whether all his permanent teeth have erupted properly. A home dental care regimen should be initiated at six months, including brushing weekly and providing good dental devices (such as nylon bones). Regular dental care promotes healthy teeth, fresh breath, and a longer life.

Dogs Older Than One Year: Continue to visit the veterinarian at least once a year. There is no such disease as "old age," but bodily functions do change with age. The eyes and ears are no longer as efficient.

Liver, kidney, and intestinal functions often decline. Proper dietary changes, recommended by your veterinarian, can make life more pleasant for your aging Labrador Retriever and you.

EVERYDAY HAPPENINGS

Keeping your Labrador Retriever healthy is a matter of keen observation and quick action when necessary. Knowing what's normal for your dog will help you recognize signs of trouble before they blossom into a full-blown emergency situation.

Even if the problem is minor, such as a cut or scrape, you'll want to care for it immediately to prevent subsequent infections, as well as to ensure that your dog doesn't make it worse by chewing or scratching at it. Here's what to do for common, minor injuries

or illnesses, and how to recognize and deal with emergencies.

Cuts and Scrapes: For a cut or scrape that's half an inch or smaller, clean the wound with saline solution or warm water and use tweezers to remove any splinters or other debris. Apply antibiotic ointment. No bandage is necessary unless the wound is on a paw, which can pick up dirt when your dog walks on it. Deep cuts with lots of bleeding or those caused by glass or some other object should be treated by your veterinarian.

Cold Symptoms: Dogs don't actually get colds, but they can get illnesses that have similar symptoms, such as coughing, a runny nose, or sneezing. Dogs cough for any number of reasons, from respiratory infections to inhaled irritants to congestive heart failure. Take your dog to the veterinarian for prolonged coughing, or coughing accompanied by labored breathing, runny eyes or nose, or bloody phlegm.

A runny nose that continues for more than several hours requires veterinary attention, as well. If your Lab sneezes, he may have some mild nasal irritation that will resolve on its own, but frequent sneezing, especially if it's accompanied by a runny nose, may indicate anything from allergies to an infection to something stuck in the nose.

Vomiting and Diarrhea: Sometimes dogs suffer minor gastric upsets when they eat a new type of food, eat too much, get into the garbage, or become excited or anxious. Give the stomach a rest by withholding food for twelve hours, and then feeding a bland diet such as baby food or rice and chicken, gradually returning the dog to his normal food. Projectile vomiting, or vomiting or diarrhea that continues for more than forty-eight hours, is another matter. Your dog should be seen by the veterinarian.

No matter how careful you are with your lovely Lab, sometimes unexpected injuries happen. Be prepared for any emergency by creating a canine first-aid kit. Find out what essentials you need on **DogChannel.com/Club-Lab**—click on "downloads."

CHAPTER 7

ON THE TOPIC

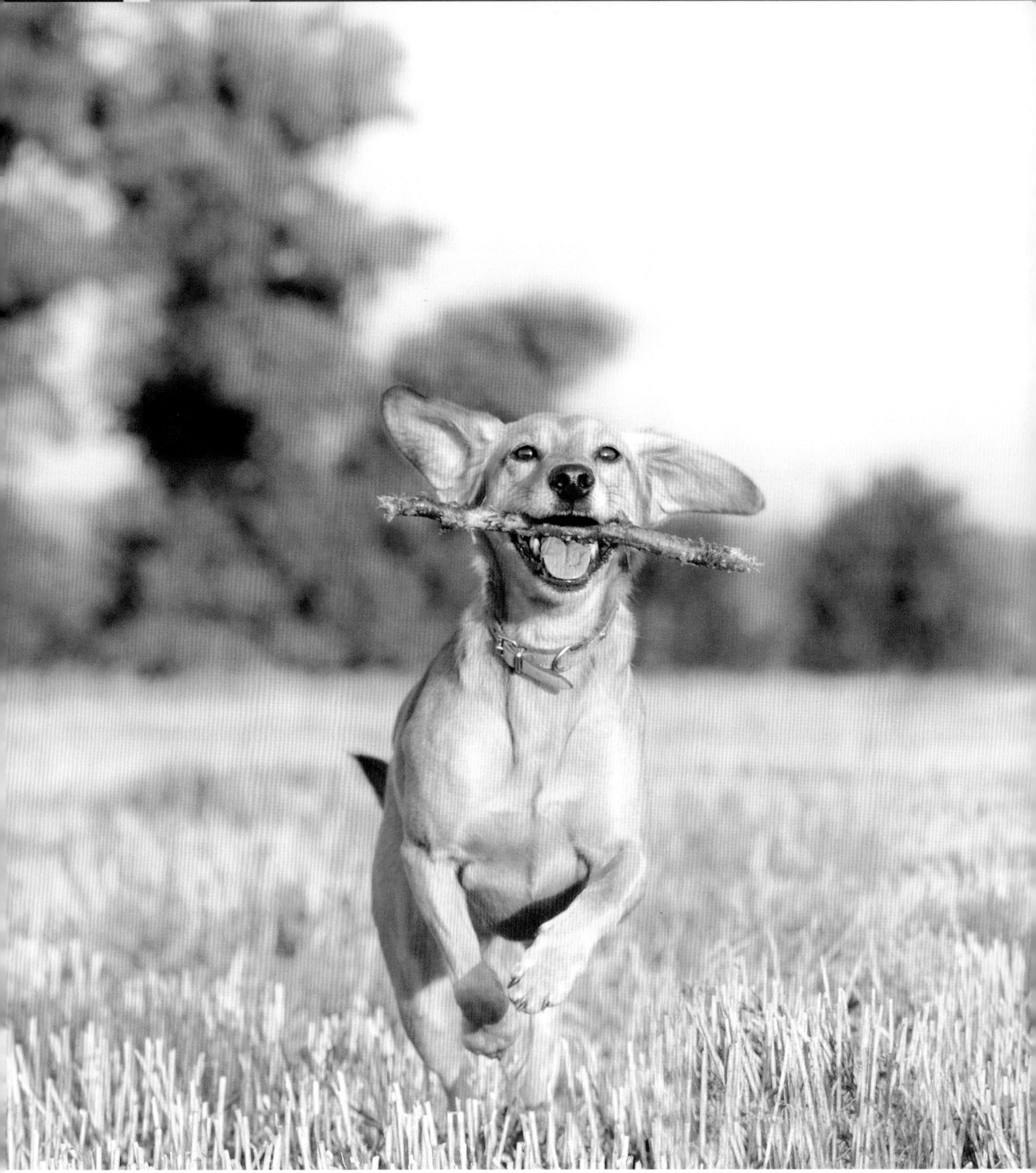

OF HEALTH

It's not always easy keeping your dog fit and healthy. Although Labrador Retrievers are generally vigorous, sturdy, healthy dogs, there are some diseases and hereditary disorders of which you should be aware.

SKIN PROBLEMS

Veterinarians are consulted by dog owners for skin problems more than for any other group of diseases or maladies. A dog's skin is as sensitive, if not more so, as human skin, and both suffer almost the same ailments (though the occurrence of acne in most breeds of dog is rare!). For this reason, veterinary dermatology has developed into a specialty practiced by many veterinarians.

Because many skin problems have visual symptoms that are almost identical, it requires the skill of an experienced veterinary dermatologist to identify and cure many of the more severe skin disorders. Pet-supply stores sell many treatments for skin problems, but most of them are directed at symptoms and not at the underlying problem(s). If your Labrador is suffering from a skin disorder, seek professional assistance as quickly as possible. As with all diseases, the earlier a problem is identified and treated, the more likely that the cure will be

it's a **Fact**

Dogs can get Lyme disease, Rocky Mountain spotted fever, tick bite paralysis, and many other diseases from ticks.

successful. There are active programs being undertaken by many veterinary pharmaceutical manufacturers to solve most, if not all, of the common skin problems in dog.

PARASITE BITES

Insect bites itch, erupt, and may even become infected. Dogs have the same reaction to fleas, ticks, and/or mites. When an insect lands on you, you have the chance to whisk it away with your hand. Unfortunately, when a dog is bitten by a flea, tick, or mite, he can only scratch it away or bite it. By the time the dog has been bitten, the parasite has done its damage. It may also have laid eggs, which will cause further problems in the future. The itching from parasite bites is probably due to the saliva injected into the site when the parasite sucks the dog's blood.

AIRBORNE ALLERGIES

Just as humans suffer from hay fever during the pollinating season, many dogs suffer from the same allergies. When the pollen count is high, your dog might suffer, but don't expect him to sneeze or have a runny nose like a human. Dogs react to pollen allergies in the same way they react to fleas; they scratch and bite themselves. Dogs, like humans, can be tested for allergens. Discuss the testing with your veterinarian.

AUTO-IMMUNE ILLNESS

An auto-immune illness is one in which the immune system overacts and does not recognize parts of the affected person. Instead, the immune system starts to react as if these parts were foreign and need to be destroyed. An example is rheumatoid arthritis, which occurs when the body does not recognize the joints, which leads to a very painful and damaging reaction in the joints. This has nothing to do with age, so it can occur in puppies. The wear-and-tear arthritis in older people or dogs is called osteoarthritis.

Lupus is another auto-immune disease that affects dogs as well as people. It can take variable forms, affecting the kidneys, bones, and the skin. It can be fatal, so it is treated with steroids, which can themselves have very significant side effects. Steroids calm down the allergic reaction to the body's tissues, which helps the lupus, but also calms down the body's reaction to real for-

SMART TIP!

For maximum health and social benefits, your Lab should be spayed (female) or neutered (male) before your youngster hits puberty. Studies found that, with altered anesthesia protocols, it's safe to perform spays and neuters on puppies as young as six weeks old, and that younger pups recover faster and with less pain than do older puppies.

eign substances such as bacteria, and also thins the skin and bones.

FOOD ALLERGIES

Feeding your dog properly is very important. An incorrect diet could affect your Lab's health, behavior, and nervous system, possibly making a normal dog an aggressive one. The result of a good—or bad—diet is most visible in a dog's skin and coat, but internal organs are affected, too.

Dogs are allergic to many foods that are popular and highly recommended by breeders and veterinarians. Changing the brand of food may not eliminate the problem if the ingredient to which your dog is allergic is contained in the new brand.

Recognizing a food allergy can be difficult. Humans often have rashes or swelling of the lips or eyes when they eat foods they are allergic to. Dogs do not usually develop rashes, but they react the same way they do to an airborne or bite allergy—they itch, scratch, and bite. While pollen allergies and parasite bites are usually seasonal, food allergies are year-round problems.

Diagnosis of a food allergy is based on a two- to four-week dietary trial with a home-cooked diet fed to the exclusion of all other foods. The diet should consist of boiled rice or potato with a source of protein that the dog has never eaten before, such as fresh or frozen fish, lamb, or even something as exotic as pheasant. Water has to be the only drink, and it is important that no other foods are fed during this trial. If your dog's condition improves, try the original diet again to see if the itching resumes. If it does, then your dog is allergic to his original diet. You must find a diet that does not distress your dog's skin. Start with a commercially available hypoallergenic diet or the homemade diet that you created for the allergy trial.

Food intolerance is the inability of the dog to completely digest certain foods. This occurs because the dog does not have the chemicals (enzymes) necessary to digest some foodstuffs. All puppies have the enzymes necessary to digest canine milk, but some dogs do not have the enzymes to digest cow milk, resulting in loose bowels, stomach pains, and the passage of gas.

Dogs often do not have the enzymes to digest soy or other beans. The treatment is to exclude these foods from your Labrador Retriever's diet.

EXTERNAL PARASITES

Fleas: Of all the problems to which dogs are prone, none is better known and more frustrating than fleas. Flea infestation is relatively simple to cure but difficult to prevent.

To control flea infestation, you have to understand the flea's life cycle. Fleas are often thought of as a summertime problem, but centrally heated homes have changed the patterns and fleas can be found at any time of the year. The most effective method of flea control is a two-stage approach: Kill the adult fleas, then control the development of pre-adult fleas. Unfortunately, no single active ingredient is effective against all stages of the flea life cycle.

Treating fleas should be a two-pronged attack. First, the environment needs to be treated; this includes carpets and furniture, especially the dog's bedding and areas underneath furniture. The environment should be treated with a household spray containing an insect growth regulator and an insecticide to kill the adult fleas. Most IGRs are effective against eggs and larvae; they actually mimic the fleas' own hormones and stop the eggs and larvae from developing into adult fleas. There are currently no treatments available to attack the pupae stage of the life cycle, so the adult insecticide is used to kill the newly hatched adult fleas before they find a host. Most IGRs are active for many months, while adult insecticides are only active for a few days.

When treating with a household spray, vacuum before applying the product. This stimulates as many pupae as possible to hatch into adult fleas. The vacuum cleaner should also be treated

with an insecticide to prevent the eggs and larvae that have been collected in the vacuum bag from hatching.

The second stage of treatment is to apply an adult insecticide to the dog. Traditionally, this would be in the form of a collar or a spray, but more recent innovations include digestible insecticides that poison the fleas when they ingest the dog's blood. Alternatively, there are drops that, when placed on the back of the dog's neck, spread throughout the hair and skin to kill adult fleas.

Ticks: Though not as common as fleas, ticks are found all over the tropical and temperate world. They don't bite like fleas; they harpoon. They dig their sharp proboscis (nose) into the dog's skin and drink the blood, which is their only food and drink. Ticks are controlled the same way fleas are controlled.

The American dog tick, *Dermacentor variabilis*, may well be the most common dog

Did You Know? Across the globe, more than 800 species of ticks exist, and they aren't particular about where they dine. Mammals, birds, and reptiles are all fair game.

tick in many geographical areas, especially those areas where the climate is hot and humid areas. Most dog ticks have life expectancies of a week to six months, depending on climatic conditions. They can neither jump nor fly, but they can crawl slowly and can range up to sixteen feet to reach a sleeping or unsuspecting dog.

Mites: Just as fleas and ticks can be problematic for your dog, mites can also lead to an itch fit. Microscopic in size, mites are related to ticks and generally take up permanent residence on their host animal—in this case, your dog! The term "mange" refers to any infestation caused by one of the mighty mites, of which there are six varieties that smart dog owners should know.

● *Demodex mites* cause a condition known as demodicosis (sometimes called "red mange" or "follicular mange"), in which the mites live in the dog's hair follicles and sebaceous glands in larger-than-normal numbers. Most dogs recover from this type of mange without any treatment, though topical therapies are commonly prescribed by the vet.

● The *Cheyletiellosis mite* is the hook-mouthed culprit associated with "walking dandruff," a condition that affects dogs as well as cats and rabbits. If untreated, this mange can affect a whole kennel of dogs and can be spread to humans, as well.

● The *Sarcoptes mite* causes intense itching on the dog in the form of a condi-

Labs are a healthy breed, and most pets won't ever have to deal with genetic illnesses.

tion known as scabies or sarcoptic mange. Scabies is highly contagious and can be passed to humans. Sometimes an allergic reaction to the mite worsens the severe itching associated with sarcoptic mange.

● Ear mites, *Otodectes cynotis*, lead to otodectic mange, which commonly affects the outer ear canal of the dog, though other areas can be affected as well. Your vet can prescribe a treatment to flush out the ears and kill any eggs in the ears. A complete month of treatment is necessary to cure the mange.

● Two other mites, less common in dogs, include *Dermanyssus gallinae* (the "poultry" or "red mite") and *Eutrombicula alfreddugesi* (the North American mite associated with trombiculidiasis or chigger infestation). The types of mange caused by both of these mites must be treated by vets.

INTERNAL PARASITES

Most animals—fishes, birds, and mammals, including dogs and humans—have worms and other parasites that live inside their bodies. According to Dr. Herbert R. Axelrod, a fish pathologist, there are two kinds of parasites: dumb and smart. The smart parasites live in peaceful cooperation with their hosts (symbiosis), while the dumb parasites kill their hosts. Most worm infections are relatively easy to control. If they are not controlled, they weaken the host dog to the point that other medical problems occur, but they do not kill the host as dumb parasites would.

Roundworms: Roundworms that infect dogs live in the dog's intestines and shed eggs continually. It has been estimated that a dog produces about six or more ounces of feces every day. Each ounce averages hundreds of thousands of roundworm eggs. There are no known areas in which dogs roam that do not contain roundworm eggs. Because roundworms infect people, too, it is wise to have your dog regularly tested.

Roundworm infection can kill puppies and cause severe problems in adult dogs, as the hatched larvae travel to the lungs and trachea through the bloodstream. Cleanliness is the best preventive for roundworms. Always pick up after your dog and dispose of feces in appropriate receptacles.

Hookworms: Hookworms are dangerous to humans as well as to dogs and cats, and can be the cause of severe anemia due to iron deficiency. The worm uses its teeth to attach itself to the dog's intestines and changes the site of its attachment about six times per day. Each time the worm repositions itself, the dog loses blood and can become anemic.

Symptoms of hookworm infection include dark stools, weight loss, general weakness, pale coloration, and anemia, as well as possible skin problems. Fortunately, hookworms are easily purged with a number of medications that have proven effective. Discuss these with your veterinarian. Most heartworm preventives include a hookworm insecticide, as well.

Humans, can be infected by hookworms, who can acquire the larvae through exposure to contaminated feces. Because the worms cannot complete their life cycle on a human, the worms simply infest the skin and cause irritation. As a preventative, use disposable gloves or a "poop-scoop" to pick up your dog's droppings and prevent your dog (or neighborhood cats) from defecating in children's play areas.

Tapeworms: There are many species of tapeworm, all of which are carried by fleas! Fleas are so small that your dog could pass them onto your hands, your plate, or your food, making it possible for you to ingest a flea that is carrying tapeworm eggs. While tapeworm infection is not life-threatening in dogs (smart parasite!), it can be the cause of a very serious liver disease in humans.

Whipworms: In North America, whipworms are counted among the most common parasitic worms in dogs. Affected dogs may only experience upset tummies, colic, and diarrhea. These worms, however, can live for months or years in the dog, beginning their larval stage in the small intestine, spending

Internal parasites are not as easy to detect, but they may make your dog feel sick.

their adult stage in the large intestine and finally passing infective eggs through the dog's feces. The only way to detect whipworms is through a fecal examination, though this is not always foolproof. Treatment for whipworms is tricky, due to the worms' unusual life cycle, and often dogs are reinfected due to exposure to infective eggs on the ground. Cleaning up droppings in your backyard as well as in public places is absolutely essential for sanitation purposes and the health of your dog and others.

Threadworms: Though less common than roundworms, hookworms, and those previously mentioned parasites, threadworms concern dog owners in southwestern United States and the Gulf Coast area where the climate is hot and humid. Living in the small intestine of the dog, this worm measures a mere 2 millimeters and is round in shape. Like the whipworm, the threadworm's life cycle is very complex, and the eggs and larvae are passed through the feces. A deadly disease in humans, threadworms readily infect people, most commonly through the handling of feces. Threadworms

are most often seen in young puppies; bloody diarrhea and pneumonia are symptoms. Sick puppies must be isolated and treated immediately; vets recommend a follow-up treatment one month later.

Heartworms: Heartworms are thin, extended worms up to 12 inches long, that live in a dog's heart and the major blood vessels surrounding it. Dogs may have up to 200 heartworms. Symptoms may be loss of energy, loss of appetite, coughing, the development of a pot belly, and anemia.

Heartworms are transmitted by mosquitoes, which drink the blood of infected dogs and take in larvae with the blood. The larvae, called *microfilariae*, develop within the body of the mosquito and are passed on to the next dog bitten after the larvae mature. It takes two to three weeks for the larvae to develop to the infective stage within the body of the mosquito.

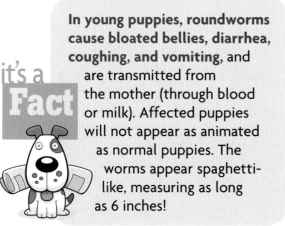

it's a Fact

In young puppies, roundworms cause bloated bellies, diarrhea, coughing, and vomiting, and are transmitted from the mother (through blood or milk). Affected puppies will not appear as animated as normal puppies. The worms appear spaghetti-like, measuring as long as 6 inches!

Dogs are usually treated at about six weeks of age and maintained on a prophylactic dose given monthly.

Blood testing for heartworms is not necessarily indicative of how seriously your dog is infected. Although this is a dangerous disease, it is not easy for a dog to be infected. Discuss the various preventives with your vet, because there are many different types now available. Together you can decide on a safe course of prevention for your dog.

HIP DYSPLASIA

The most common heritable orthopedic disease in dogs is chronic hip dysplasia, a condition where the hip joint becomes deformed, resulting in a loose hip joint and abnormal rubbing of the joint surfaces. This rubbing eventually causes inflammation and pain, leading to arthritis. Signs include: limping, difficulty getting up, stiffness, and altered gait.

Conservative management for mildly dysplastic dogs includes weight control; pain management (anti-inflammatories under veterinary supervision); nutraceuticals (glucosamine/chondroitin combination) to promote joint health; and regular exercise to maintain muscle tone, strength, and range of motion in the joint (but not to the point where the exercise causes stiffness or lameness). More severely affected dogs may need surgical hip repair, hip reconstruction, or total hip replacement.

If diagnosed before a puppy reaches fourteen to twenty weeks of age, a simple, minimally invasive procedure known as juvenile pubic symphysidesis can be performed (often in combination with an early spay or neuter); with this procedure, growing cartilage cells in the lower pelvis are cauterized to create a tighter hip joint.

The prognosis varies, depending upon treatment option and severity of the disease. Mildly affected canines often can be successfully managed with conservative treatment for a long time. The outlook for hip repair and reconstruction generally ranges from good to excellent, while results for JPS and hip replacement usually are excellent.

Keeping your dog healthy includes getting him the proper vaccines.

Although hip dysplasia has genetic components, other factors including overfeeding and over- or under-supplementation of carbohydrates, calcium, and phosphorous in growing dogs also contribute to chronic hip dysplasia. Talk with your breeder or veterinarian to find the appropriate diet formula for your puppy or young dog.

SMART TIP! **Obesity is linked to the earlier onset of age-related health problems.** Help keep the weight off by providing your Lab with sufficient exercise and play, and by feeding proper serving sizes. Caloric requirements decline as your puppy reaches adulthood, dropping twenty-five to thirty percent within a couple of months after spaying or neutering; reduce serving portions and/or switch to a less calorie-dense diet, as needed.

ELBOW DYSPLASIA

Elbow dysplasia refers to various malformations of the elbow joint, which lead to cartilage damage, inflammation, pain, and arthritis. Signs include front leg lameness and joint swelling.

"Early surgical intervention to correct defects in the elbow joint offers the best opportunity to keep the dog doing better for a longer period of time," says Darryl Millis, D.V.M., professor of orthopedic surgery at the University of Tennessee in Knoxville. Total elbow replacement is another surgical option, although it's only performed at a few referral centers. Mild cases sometimes can be managed with weight control, glucosamine/chondroitin supplements, or pain medications.

Depending on how early treatment is initiated, the type of surgery performed, and the severity of the condition, many dogs become pain-free after surgery; others will need intermittent or permanent medication. However, because the joint is malformed, many dogs will eventually end up with arthritis later in life and will need lifelong management techniques, Millis says.

SEIZURES

Idiopathic epilepsy refers to recurrent seizures that are not a consequence of other disorders (e.g., head trauma, low blood sugar, poisoning, heart disease, kidney or liver failure, electrolyte imbalances, etc.). Because there is no diagnostic test for epilepsy, diagnosis is made by eliminating other possible causes.

Seizures typically start when dogs are between one and five years old, and can vary in presentation. "Most commonly, the dog falls to the ground with the limbs extended for a minute or so," says William Thomas, D.V.M., associate professor of neurology and neurosurgery at the University of Tennessee. "The dog then exhibits rhythmic jerking or paddling of the limbs and chewing movements, and often urinates or defecates. The entire seizure usually lasts several minutes, after which the dog is often confused and uncoordinated for a period of time." Other signs include howling, drooling, jaw chomping, and unconsciousness.

Sometimes seizures last more than five minutes or occur in multiple episodes within a short period of time. This is an emergency situation requiring immediate veterinary attention to avoid brain damage or death.

Although there is no cure, most cases can be managed and seizure activity reduced. "However, the prognosis is more guarded for dogs who suffer lengthy episodes or frequent seizures," Thomas warns. "If the seizures are not well-controlled within six months of treatment or if the diagnosis is unclear, referral to a board-certified veterinary neurologist should be considered."

It's not unusual for pups to be born with certain types of internal parasites; they get these while they are still in their mother's womb.

DOG'S SUPPER

Today, the choices of food for your Labrador Retriever are many and varied. There are dozens of brands of food in all sorts of flavors and textures, ranging from puppy diets to those for seniors. There are even hypoallergenic and low-calorie diets available.

Because your Labrador Retriever's food has a bearing on coat, health, and temperament, it is essential that the most suitable diet is selected for a Labrador Retriever of his age. It is fair to say, however, that even experienced owners can be perplexed by the enormous range of foods available. Only understanding what is best for your dog will help you reach an informed decision.

BASIC TYPES

Dog foods are produced in three basic types: dry, wet (canned), and semimoist. Dry foods are useful for the cost-conscious, because they tend to be less expensive than semimoist or canned. They also contain the least fat and the most preservatives. Dry food is the least expensive commercially available dog food. It's bulky and takes longer to eat than other foods, so it's more filling.

it's a **Fact** Bones can cause gastrointestinal obstruction and perforation, and may be contaminated with salmonella or E. coli. Leave them in the trash and give your dog a nylon toy bone instead.

Wet food—available in cans or foil pouches—is more expensive than dry food, and are made up of sixty to seventy percent water.

A palatable source of concentrated nutrition, wet food makes a good supplement for underweight dogs or those recovering from an illness. Some owners add a little wet food to dry food to increase its appeal.

Semimoist food is flavorful but usually contains lots of sugar, which can lead to dental problems and obesity. Even though most dogs like semimoist food, it's not a good choice for your Lab's main diet.

There is a fourth type of dog food, but it is less popular: Frozen food is available in cooked and raw forms, and is usually more expensive than wet foods. Frozen food can be stored for at least one year in the freezer. Longer storage can cause deterioration of the quality and taste of the food. Thaw frozen food in the refrigerator or use the defrost setting on your microwave. Cover and refrigerate leftovers, then use within 24 hours.

The amount of food your Labrador Retriever needs depends on a number of factors, such as age, activity level, food quality, reproductive status, and size. What's the easiest way to figure it out? Start with the manufacturer's recommended amount, then adjust it according to your dog's response. For example, if you feed the recommended amount for a few weeks, and your Labrador Retriever loses weight, increase the amount by ten to twenty percent. If your dog gains weight, decrease the amount. It won't take long to determine the amount of food that keeps your furry friend in optimal condition.

NUTRITION 101

All Labrador Retrievers (and all dogs, for that matter) need proteins, carbohydrates, fats, vitamins, and minerals for optimal growth and health.

■ **Proteins** are used for growth and repair of muscles, bones, and other bodily tissues. They're also used for production of antibodies, enzymes, and hormones. All dogs need protein, but it's especially important for puppies because they grow and develop so

Labs are chowhounds and usually love to indulge in anything edible. Just be sure the food they're eating is providing him with the proper nutrients.

rapidly. Protein sources include various types of meat, meat meal, meat byproducts, eggs, dairy products, and soybeans.

■ **Carbohydrates** are metabolized into glucose, the body's principal energy source. Carbohydrates are available as sugars, starches, and fiber.

• Sugars (simple carbohydrates) are not suitable nutrient sources for dogs.

• Starches—a preferred type of carbohydrate in dog food—

are found in a variety of plant products. Starches must be cooked in order to be digested.

• Fiber (cellulose)—also a preferred type of carbohydrates in dog food—isn't digestible, but helps the digestive tract function properly.

■ **Fats** are also used for energy and play an important role in skin and coat health, hormone production, nervous system function, and vitamin transport. Fat increases the palatability and the calorie count of puppy/

Believe it or not, during your Lab's lifetime, you'll buy a few thousand pounds of dog food! Go to **DogChannel.com/Club-Lab** and download a chart that outlines the cost of dog food.

dog food, which can lead to serious health problems, such as obesity, for puppies or dogs who are allowed to overindulge. Some foods contain added amounts of omega fatty acids such as docosohexaenoic acid, a compound that may enhance brain development and learning in puppies but is not considered an essential nutrient by the Association of American Feed Control Officials (www.aafco. org). Fats used in dog foods include tallow, lard, poultry fat, fish oil, and vegetable oils.

■ **Vitamins** and **minerals** participate in muscle and nerve function, bone growth, healing, metabolism, and fluid balance. Especially important for your puppy are calcium, phosphorus, and vitamin D, which must be supplied in the right balance to ensure proper development of bones and teeth.

Just as your dog needs proper nutrition from his food, water is an essential nutrient, as well. Water keeps the dog's body properly hydrated and promotes normal function of the body's systems. During house-training, it is necessary to keep an eye on how much water your Labrador Retriever is drinking, but once he is reliably trained, he should have access to clean, fresh water at all times, especially if you feed him dry food. Make sure that the dog's water bowl is clean, and change the water often.

CHECK OUT THE LABEL

To help you get a feel for what you are feeding your dog, start by taking a look at the label on the package or can. Look for the words "complete and balanced." This tells

Dogs of all ages love treats and table food, but these goodies can unbalance your retriever's diet and lead to a weight problem if you don't choose and feed them wisely. Table food, whether fed as a treat or as part of a meal, shouldn't account for more than ten percent of your Lab's daily caloric intake. If you plan to give your Lab treats, be sure to include "treat calories" when calculating the daily food requirement—so you don't end up with a pudgy pup!

When shopping for packaged treats, look for ones that provide complete nutrition—they're basically dog food in a fun form. Choose crunchy goodies for chewing fun and dental health. Other ideas for tasty treats include:

✓ small chunks of cooked, lean meat
✓ dry dog food morsels
✓ cheese
✓ veggies (cooked, raw or frozen)
✓ breads, crackers, or dry cereal
✓ unsalted, unbuttered, plain, popped popcorn

Some foods, however, can be dangerous and even deadly to a dog. The following items can cause digestive upset (vomiting or diarrhea) or toxic reactions that could be fatal:

✗ **avocados:** can cause gastrointestinal irritation, with vomiting and diarrhea, if eaten in sufficient quantity

✗ **baby food:** may contain onion powder; does not provide balanced nutrition

✗ **chocolate:** contains methylxanthines and theobromine, caffeine-like compounds that can cause vomiting, diarrhea, heart abnormalities, tremors, seizures, and death. Darker chocolates contain higher levels of the toxic compounds.

✗ **eggs, raw:** whites contain an enzyme that prevents uptake of biotin, a B vitamin; may contain salmonella

✗ **garlic (and related foods):** can cause gastrointestinal irritation and anemia if eaten in sufficient quantity

✗ **grapes:** can cause kidney failure if eaten in sufficient quantity (the toxic dose varies from dog to dog)

✗ **macadamia nuts:** can cause vomiting, weakness, lack of coordination, and other problems.

✗ **meat, raw:** may contain harmful bacteria such as salmonella or E. coli

✗ **milk:** can cause diarrhea in some puppies.

✗ **onions (and related foods):** can cause gastrointestinal irritation and anemia if eaten in sufficient quantity

✗ **raisins:** can cause kidney failure if eaten in sufficient quantity (the toxic dose varies from dog to dog)

✗ **yeast bread dough:** can rise in the gastrointestinal tract, causing obstruction; produces alcohol as it rises

All dogs need the proper amounts of protein, carbs, fats, vitamins, and minerals to be healthy.

you that the food meets specific nutritional requirements set by the AAFCO for either adults ("maintenance") or puppies and pregnant/lactating females ("growth and reproduction"). The label must state the group for which it is intended.

The label also includes a nutritional analysis, listing minimum protein and fat, maximum fiber and moisture content, as well as other information. (You won't find carbohydrate content, because it's everything that isn't protein, fat, fiber, and moisture.)

The nutritional analysis refers to crude protein and crude fat—amounts that have been determined in the laboratory. This analysis is technically accurate, but it doesn't tell you anything about digestibility: how much of the particular nutrient your Labrador Retriever can actually use. For information about digestibility, contact the manufacturer (check the label for a telephone number and website address).

Virtually all commercial puppy foods exceed AAFCO's minimal requirements for protein and fat, the two nutrients most commonly evaluated when comparing foods. Protein levels in dry puppy foods usually range from about twenty-six to thirty per-

Dry dog food (aka kibble) is the least expensive and usually most nutritious food for dogs.

SMART TIP!

How can you tell if your Lab is fit or fat?

When you run your hands down your pal's sides from front to back, you should be able to easily feel his ribs. It's OK if you feel a little body fat (and, of course, a lot of hair), but you should not feel huge fat pads. You should also be able to feel your Lab's waist —an indentation behind the ribs.

cent; for canned foods, the values are about nine to thirteen percent. The fat content of dry puppy foods is about twenty percent or more; for canned foods, it's eight percent or more. (Dry food values are larger than canned food values because dry food contains less water; the values are actually similar when compared on a dry matter basis.)

Finally, check the label's ingredient list, which lists the ingredients in descending order by weight. Manufacturers are allowed to list separately different forms of a single ingredient (e.g., ground corn and corn gluten meal). The food may contain things like meat byproducts, meat, bone meal, and animal fat, which probably won't appeal to you but are nutritious and safe for your dog. Higher quality foods usually have meat or meat products near the top of the ingredient list, but you don't need to worry about grain products as long as the label indicates that the food is nutritionally complete. Dogs are omnivores (not carnivores, as commonly believed), so all balanced dog foods contain animal and plant ingredients.

STAGES OF LIFE

When selecting your Lab's diet, three stages of development must be considered: the puppy stage, the adult stage, and the senior stage.

Puppy Diets: Puppies instinctively want milk from their mother, and a normal puppy will exhibit this behavior from just a few moments following birth. Puppies should be allowed to nurse from their mothers for about the first six weeks, although from the third or fourth week the breeder will begin to introduce small portions of suitable solid food. Most breeders like to alternate between milk and meat meals initially, building up to weaning time.

By the time puppies are seven- or a maximum of eight-weeks old, they should be fully weaned and fed solely on a proprietary puppy food. Selection of the most suitable, quality foods at this time is essential, for a puppy's fastest growth rate is during the first year of life. Veterinarians are usually able to offer advice in this regard. The frequency of meals will be reduced over time, and when a young Lab has reached the age of about ten to twelve months, he should be switched to an adult diet.

Puppy and junior diets can be balanced for the needs of your dog so that, except in certain circumstances, additional vitamins, minerals, and proteins will not be required.

Adult Diets: A dog is considered an adult when he has stopped growing. In general the diet of a Lab can be changed to an adult one at about nine to twelve months of age.

Did You Know?

Because semimoist food contains lots of sugar, it isn't a good selection for your Lab's main menu. However, it is great for an occasional yummy snack. Try forming it into little meatballs for a once-a-week treat! He'll love ya for it!

Again, you should rely on your veterinarian or dietary specialist to recommend an acceptable maintenance diet. Major dog food manufacturers specialize in this type of food, so all a smart owner needs to do is select the one best suited to his dog's needs.

Monitor your Labrador Retrievers' diet. Neutered Labrador Retrievers are twice as prone to obesity as unaltered dogs and should be fed a reduced-calorie food. Owners should consider not leaving the Labrador Retriever's food out all day for "free-choice" feeding, as this freedom inevitably translates to inches around the Labrador Retriever's waist.

Senior Diets: As dogs get older, their metabolism changes. The older dog usually exercises less, moves more slowly and sleeps more. This change in lifestyle and physiological performance requires a change in diet. Because these changes take place slowly, they might not be recognizable. These metabolic changes increase the tendency toward obesity, requiring an even more vigilant approach to feeding. Obesity in an older dog exacerbates the health problems that already accompany old age.

As your dog gets older, few of his organs function up to par. The kidneys slow down and the intestines become less efficient. These age-related factors are best handled with a change in diet and a change in feeding schedule to give smaller portions that are more easily digested.

There is no single best diet for every older dog. While many dogs do well on light or senior diets, other dogs do better on puppy diets or other special premium diets such as lamb and rice. Be sensitive to your senior Labrador Retriever's diet, which will help control other problems that may arise with your old friend.

GASTRIC DILATATION-VOLVULUS

Gastric dilatation-volvulus (also known as GDV or "bloat") is a feeding-related disorder that most commonly affects large, deep-chested dogs. As the name indicates, the disorder has two components: gastric dilatation (an excessive accumulation of gas and fluid in the stomach) and volvulus (a twisting of the stomach, which can occur if the dilatation is not relieved).

The most prominent sign of GDV is a severely distended abdomen that sounds like a drum when tapped. Afflicted dogs are restless and uncomfortable and may vomit without bringing anything up. The disorder worsens rapidly; prompt veterinary attention is required to prevent circulatory collapse (shock) and death. Home remedies for GDV aren't effective.

Several factors increase a dog's risk of developing GDV, including deep-chested conformation; having a parent, sibling, or offspring affected by GDV; age (older dogs are more susceptible); a nervous personality; rapid eating; large meals; high-fat foods; meals composed solely of dry food; and eating from a raised dish. Despite the common belief that water consumption during or after eating, and exercise after eating can cause GDV, the role of these factors has not been clearly demonstrated.

To reduce the risk of GDV, feed your Lab a combination of dry and canned food (not high-fat) from a dish placed on the floor. Encourage slower eating by feeding at least twice a day. If necessary, put an 8- to 10-inch piece of sturdy chain (1-inch links) in the food bowl; your Lab will have to slow down to pick the food from around the chain. Also, avoid stressful situations either before or after mealtime.

These delicious, dog-friendly recipes will have your furry friend smacking his lips and salivating for more. Just remember: Treats aren't meant to replace your dog's regular meals. Give your dog snacks sparingly and continue to feed her nutritious, well-balanced meals.

Cheddar Squares

$1/3$ cup all-natural applesauce
$1/3$ cup low-fat cheddar cheese, shredded
$1/3$ cup water
2 cups unbleached white flour

In a medium bowl, mix all wet ingredients. In a large bowl, mix all dry ingredients. Slowly add the wet ingredients to the dry mixture. Mix well. Pour batter into a greased 13x9x2-inch pan. Bake at 375-degrees Fahrenheit for 25 to 30 minutes. Bars are done when a toothpick inserted in the center and removed comes out clean. Cool and cut into bars. Makes about 54 one-and-a-half-inch bars.

Peanut Butter Bites

3 tablespoons vegetable oil
$1/4$ cup smooth peanut butter, no salt or sugar
$1/4$ cup honey
$1 1/2$ teaspoon baking powder
2 eggs
2 cups whole wheat flower

In a large bowl, mix all ingredients until dough is firm. If the dough is too sticky, mix in a small amount of flour. Knead dough on a lightly floured surface until firm. Roll out dough half an inch thick and cut with cookie cutters. Put cookies on a cookie sheet half an inch apart. Bake at 350-degrees Fahrenheit for 20 to 25 minutes. When done, cookies should be firm to the touch. Turn oven off and leave cookies for one to two hours to harden. Makes about 40 two-inch-long cookies.

Labrador Retrievers do not require elaborate haircuts or a lot of finishing work. Basically, the main goal in grooming your Lab is to keep his coat looking nice and in good health. During shedding season in the spring, you will need to pay a little more attention to his coat, but a vigorous brushing will loosen much of the dead hair in the undercoat. Follow up with a metal comb to remove the hair that is being cast off.

Some owners like to emphasize the otter-like look of the Labrador's tail by trimming it to give it a blunt point. Spray-on coat gloss is another optional grooming tool; this will give the Labrador's short, dense coat a sleek sheen. An extra-shiny coat looks especially nice on black dogs.

A slicker brush, pin brush, or metal comb can be used for routine grooming. Daily brushing is effective for removing dead hair and stimulating the dog's natural oils to add shine and a healthy look to the coat. Your Labrador Retriever is not a breed that needs excessive grooming, but his coat needs to be brushed daily as part of regular maintenance. Daily brushing will minimize mats,

Did You Know? Nail clipping can be tricky, so many dog owners leave the task for the professionals. However, if you walk your dog on concrete, you may not have to worry about it. The concrete acts like a nail file and will probably keep the nails in check.

get rid of dust and dandruff, and remove any dead hair. Regular grooming sessions also are a good way to spend time with your dog. Many dogs grow to like the feel of being brushed and will enjoy the daily routine.

BATHING

Dogs do not need to be bathed as often as humans, but occasional bathing is important for healthy skin and a shiny coat. Again, like most anything, if you accustom your pup to being bathed as a puppy, it will be second nature by the time he grows up. You want your dog to be at ease in the bath or else it could end up a wet, soapy, messy ordeal for both of you! Your Lab should take to water almost instantly, making bathing easier.

Brush your Labrador Retriever thoroughly before wetting his coat. This will get rid of most debris and dead hairs, which are more difficult to remove when the coat is wet. Make sure that your Lab has a good nonslip surface to stand on. Begin by wetting the dog's coat. A shower or hose attachment is necessary for thoroughly wetting and rinsing the coat. Check the water temperature to make sure that it is neither too hot nor too cold.

Next, apply shampoo to the dog's coat and work it into a good lather. You should purchase a soap-free shampoo that is made for dogs; do not use a product that's made for human hair. Wash the head last; you do not want shampoo to drip into the dog's eyes while you are washing the rest of his body. Work the shampoo all the way down to the skin. You can use this opportunity to check the skin for any bumps, bites, or other abnormalities. Do not neglect any area of the body—get all of the hard-to-reach places.

Once the dog has been shampooed, he requires an equally thorough rinsing. Shampoo left in the coat can be irritating to the

Labs don't need to be bathed very often; only when they have a run-in with a mud puddle or start to smell "doggie."

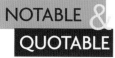
After removing a tick, clean the dog's skin with hydrogen peroxide. If Lyme disease is common where you live, have your veterinarian test the tick. Tick preventative medication will discourage ticks from attaching and kill any that do.

—groomer Andrea Vilardi from West Paterson, N.J.

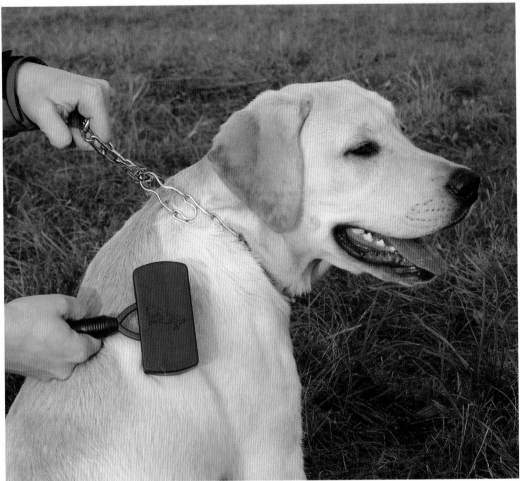

Moderate shedders, Labs should be brushed on a regular basis.

skin. Protect his eyes from the shampoo by shielding them with your hand and directing the flow of water in the opposite direction. You should also avoid getting water in the ear canal. Be prepared for your Lab to shake out his coat—you might want to stand back, but make sure you have a hold on the dog to keep him from running through the house.

it's a Fact

The short, "otter" tail of the Labrador Retriever aids him in swimming.

EAR CLEANING

Your Lab's ears should be kept clean and any excess hair inside the ear should be trimmed. Ears can be cleaned with a cotton ball and special cleaner or ear powder made for dogs.

Be on the lookout for any signs of infection or ear-mite infestation. If your Labrador Retriever has been shaking his head or scratching at his ears frequently, this usually indicates that there is a problem. If his ears have an unusual odor, this is a sure sign of mite infestation or infection, and a signal to have his ears checked by the vet.

NOTABLE & QUOTABLE

It's very important to not overbathe your Labrador and never use [human] soap or shampoo on his coat. If he happens to roll in something smelly, rinsing the coat with [plain] water usually takes care of it.—Linda Maffett, a Lab breeder in Bellingham, Wash.

Proper grooming not only will make your Lab look nice, but it will make him feel great, too!

NAIL CLIPPING

Periodic nail trimming can be done during the brushing routine. Your veterinarian will teach you how to cut your Lab's nails without cutting the "quick" (the blood vessels that run through the center of each nail and grow rather close to the end).

Your Labrador Retriever should be accustomed to having his nails trimmed at an early age, because it will be part of your maintenance routine throughout his life. Not only does it look nicer, but long nails can scratch someone unintentionally. Also, a long nail has a better chance of ripping and bleeding, or causing the feet to spread. A good rule of thumb is that if you can hear your dog's nails' clicking on the floor when he walks, his nails are too long.

Before you start cutting, make sure you can identify the quick in each nail. It will bleed if accidentally cut, which will be quite painful for the dog as it contains nerve endings. Keep some type of clotting agent on hand, such as a styptic pencil or styptic powder (the type used for shaving). This will rapidly stop the bleeding when applied to the end of the cut nail. Do not panic if this happens; just stop the bleeding and talk soothingly to your Labrador. Once he has calmed down, move on to the next nail. It is better to take it slowly and clip a little at a time, particularly with black-nailed dogs.

Hold your pup steady as you begin trimming his nails; you do not want him to make any sudden movements or run away. Talk to him soothingly and stroke him as you clip. Holding his foot in your hand, simply take off the end of each nail in one

SMART TIP!

Treats are useful in encouraging correct behavior, such as standing for grooming or nail trimming.

quick clip. You can purchase nail clippers that are specially made for dogs; you can probably find them wherever you buy grooming supplies.

There are two predominant types of clippers. One is the guillotine clipper, which is a hole with a blade in the middle. Squeeze the handles, and the blade meets the nail

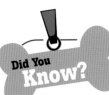
Did You Know?

Dogs can't rinse and spit after a brushing, so dog toothpaste must be safe for pets to swallow. Always use a toothpaste specially formulated for dogs when brushing your Labrador Retriever's teeth.

and chops it off. Sounds gruesome, and for some dogs, it is intolerable. Scissor-type clippers are gentler on the nail. Make sure the blades on either of these clippers are sharp.

Once you are at the desired length, use a nail file to smooth the rough edges of the nails so they don't catch on carpeting or debris outdoors.

DENTAL CARE

Like people, Labrador Retrievers can suffer from dental disease, so experts recommend regular tooth brushing. Daily brushing is best, but your dog will benefit from tooth brushing a few times a week. The teeth should be white and free of yellowish tartar,

When your pup is active outdoors, be sure to give him a quick wipe down to remove any excess sand, dirt, grit, or thorns that may have stuck to him while playing.

and the gums should appear healthy and pink. Gums that bleed easily when you perform dental duties may have gingivitis.

The first thing to know is that your puppy might not appreciate your fingers in his mouth. Desensitizing your Lab puppy—getting him to accept that you will be looking at and touching his teeth—is the first step to overcoming his reticence. You can begin this as soon as you get your puppy, with the help of the thing that motivates him most: food.

For starters, let your puppy lick some chicken, vegetable, or beef broth off your finger. Then, dip your finger in broth again, and gently insert your finger in the side of your Labrador's mouth. Touch his side teeth

Did You Know? The crunchiness of unmoistened dry dog food helps keep teeth healthy by reducing plaque accumulation and massaging the gums.

and gums. Several sessions will get your puppy used to having his mouth touched.

Use a toothbrush that is specifically made for a dog or a finger-tip brush wrapped around your finger to brush your Labrador Retriever's teeth. Hold the mouth with the fingers of one hand, and brush with the other. Use toothpaste made specifically for dogs with dog-slurping flavors like poultry and beef. The human kind froths too much and can give your dog an upset stomach. Brush in a circular motion with the brush held at a forty-five-degree angle to the gum line. Be sure to get the fronts, tops, and sides of each tooth.

Look for signs of plaque, tartar, or gum disease, including redness, swelling, foul breath, discolored enamel near the gum line, and receding gums. If you see these, take

Funny Bone

Q. Where should you never take your Labrador Retriever?
A. To the flea market!

your dog to the veterinarian immediately. Also, take your Lab to the vet once a year for a dental checkup.

THE GREAT OUTDOORS

Labrador Retrievers' prowess as hunting dogs is well known, so it's not surprising to find them at work in the great outdoors. Of course, field work has it rewards, but it also

Labs are naturally good-looking dogs, and require little to look snazzy.

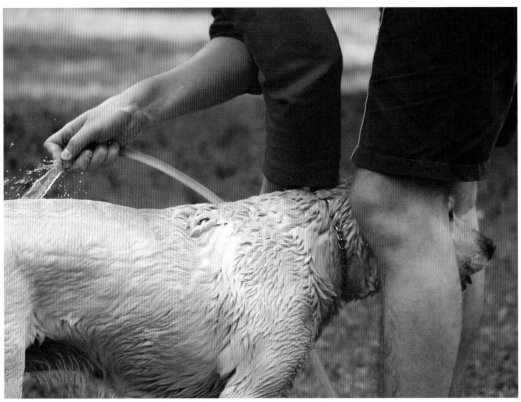

When bathing your dog, scrub his back first (right), then work your way to his head (opposite page).

has a few hazards. Lab owners should keep a sharp eye out for the various pests that their dogs may encounter out in the field.

One hazard that is very obvious is the dreaded porcupine quill. If your Lab gets "quilled," you will have to decide whether to pullout the quills yourself or visit your veterinarian.

If your dog only has a few quills and you're certain that there are none in his mouth, throat, or nose, you can remove them yourself using pliers. It's a good idea to cover your dog's eyes first so that he can't watch the procedure. Using the pliers, firmly grab the quill close to the skin and pull it straight out. For a large number of quills or for any quills that are deeply embedded in the mouth, ears, or nose, take your Lab to a veterinarian immediately for removal.

In addition, even if you remove the quills yourself, it's still a good idea to visit your veterinarian in case antibiotics are needed.

Your Lab also could get sprayed by a skunk. There will be no mistaking the lovely odor of this black-and-white critter. If your Lab has the bad fortune to get sprayed, the first thing to do is make sure that, despite the smell, your dog is physically OK. Next, assess where most of the spray hit your dog. If he got blasted in the eyes and nose, a trip to the veterinarian is called for. You can gently wipe around the eyes and nose with a damp cloth, but skunk spray in the eyes is extremely painful and should be treated by a veterinarian. If you think your Lab may have been scratched by a skunk, make sure his rabies shot is up to date. As for the smell, here is a remedy to try:

■ Use one quart of three percent hydrogen peroxide, one-quarter cup of baking soda and one teaspoon liquid soap. Mix the ingredients in a large container. This liquid will fizz. Soak your Lab's fur, being careful not to get any of the solution in his eyes.

After massaging the mixture into his fur, rinse thoroughly. Repeat if necessary.

Other grooming nuisances include burrs, stickers and fox tails. Check in and around your Lab's ears and in between the pads of her paws for burrs and stickers.

For people living west of the Mississippi, foxtails are a nuisance that must be dealt with as soon as possible. This barbed seed can become lodged anywhere on your dog's body, but appears most commonly between his toes or in his ears. If you find a foxtail, pull it out. The best way to prevent a foxtail from becoming embedded in your dog and causing an infection is early detection and removal.

TRAIN

Reward-based training methods—clicker and luring—show dogs what to do and help them do it correctly, setting them up for success and rewards rather than mistakes and punishment. Most dogs find food rewards meaningful; Labs are no exception. They tend to be very food-motivated.

Positive training relies on using treats, at least initially, to encourage the dog to offer a behavior. The treat is then given as a reward. When you reinforce desired behaviors with rewards that are valuable to the dog, you are met with happy cooperation, rather than resistance.

Positive does not mean permissive. While you are rewarding your Lab's desirable behaviors, you must manage him to be sure he doesn't get rewarded for undesirable behaviors. Training tools, such as leashes, tethers, baby gates, and crates, help keep your dog out of trouble, and the use of force-free negative punishment (the dog's behavior makes a good thing go away) helps him realize there are negative consequences for inappropriate behaviors.

Did You Know?

The prime period for socialization is short. Most behavorial experts agree that positive experiences during the ten-week period between four and fourteen weeks of age are vital to the development of a puppy who'll grow into an adult dog with a sound temperament.

LEARNING SOCIAL GRACES

Now that you have done all of the preparatory work and have helped your pup get accustomed to his new home and family, it is time for you to have some fun! Socializing your Labrador pup gives you the opportunity to show off your new friend, and your pup gets to reap the benefits of being an adorable little creature that people will want to pet and, in general, think is absolutely precious!

Besides getting to know his new family, your puppy should be exposed to other people, animals, and situations, but not until he has had all his vaccinations. This will help your Labrador Retriever become well adjusted as he grows up, and less prone to being timid or fearful of the new things he will encounter.

Your puppy's socialization began at the breeder's home, but now it is your responsibility to continue it. The socialization he

receives up until the age of twelve weeks is the most critical, as this is the time when he forms his impressions of the outside world. Be especially careful during the eight- to ten-week period, also known as the fear period. The interaction your Lab receives during this time should be gentle and reassuring. Lack of socialization can manifest itself in fear and aggression as the dog grows up. The pup needs lots of human contact, affection, handling, and exposure to other animals.

Once your pup has received his necessary vaccinations, feel free to take him out and

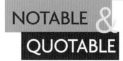

If you want to make your dog happy, create a digging spot where he's allowed to disrupt the earth. Encourage him to dig there by burying bones and toys, and helping him dig them up.

—Pat Miller, a certified pet dog trainer and owner of Peaceable Paws dog-training facility in Hagerstown, Md.

about (on his leash, of course). Walk him around the neighborhood, take him on your daily errands, let people pet him, and let him meet other dogs and pets. Make sure to expose your Lab to different people—men, women, kids, babies, men with beards, teenagers with cell phones or riding skateboards, joggers, shoppers, someone in a wheelchair, a pregnant woman, etc. Make sure your Lab explores different surfaces like sidewalks, gravel, and puddles. Positive experience is the key to building confidence. It's up to you make sure your Lab safely discovers the world so he will be a calm, confident, and well-socialized dog.

It's very important that you take the lead in all socialization experiences and never put your puppy in a scary or potentially harmful situation. Be mindful of your Labrador Retriever's limitations. Fifteen minutes at a public market is fine; two hours at a loud outdoor concert is probably too much. Meeting vaccinated, tolerant, and gentle older dogs is great. Meeting dogs

SMART TIP! **If your Lab puppy refuses to sit** with both haunches squarely beneath him and instead sits on one side or the other, he may have a physical reason for doing so. Discuss the habit with your veterinarian to be certain that your dog isn't suffering from some structural problem.

you don't know isn't such a great idea, especially if they appear very energetic, dominant, or fearful. Control the situations in which you place your puppy.

The best way to socialize your puppy to a new experience is to make him think it's the best thing ever. You can do this with a lot of talk, enthusiasm, and, yes, food.

To convince your puppy that almost any experience is fun, always carry treats. Consider carrying two types—a bag of his puppy chow, which you can give him when introducing him to nonthreatening

At a minimum, your dog should know how to sit, stay, lie down, and come on cue.

experiences, and a bag of high-value, mouth-watering treats—such as boiled chicken pieces—to give him when introducing to scarier experiences.

BASIC CUES

All Labrador Retrievers, regardless of your training and relationship goals, need to know at least five basic good-manner behaviors: sit, down, stay, come, and heel. Here are tips for teaching your dog these important cues.

Sit: Every dog should learn how to sit on command.

▲ Hold a treat at the end of your Labrador Retriever's nose.

▲ Move the treat over his head.

▲ When your dog sits, click a clicker or say "Yes!"

▲ Feed your dog the treat.

▲ If your dog jumps up, hold the treat lower. If he backs up, back him into a corner and wait until he sits. Be patient. Keep your clicker handy, and click (or say "Yes!") and treat anytime he offers a sit.

▲ When he easily offers sits, say "sit" just before he offers, so he can make the association between the word and the behavior. Add the sit cue when you know you can get the behavior. Your dog doesn't know what the word means until you repeatedly associate it with the appropriate behavior.

▲ When your Lab sits easily on cue, start using intermittent reinforcement by clicking some sits but not others. At first, click most sits and skip an occasional one (this is a high rate of reinforcement). Gradually make your clicks more and more random.

Down: If your dog can sit, then he can learn to lie down.

▼ Have your dog sit.

▼ Hold the treat in front of his nose. Move it down slowly, straight toward the floor (toward his toes). If he follows all the way down, click and treat.

▼ If he gets stuck, move the treat down more slowly. Click and treat for small movements downward—moving his head a bit lower, or inching one paw forward. Keep clicking and treating until he is all the way down. This is called "shaping"— rewarding small pieces of a behavior until your dog succeeds.

▼ If your Labrador Retriever stands as you move the treat toward the floor, have him sit, and move the treat more slowly downward, shaping with clicks and treats for small movement down as long as he is sitting. If he stands, cheerfully say "Oops!" (which means "Sorry, no treat for that!"), have him sit, and try again.

Once your dog knows the basic cues, it will be easier to teach him more advanced things like tricks.

▼ If shaping isn't working, sit on the floor with your knee raised. Have your Lab sit next to you. Put your hand with the treat under your knee and lure him under your leg so that he lies down and crawls to follow the treat. Click and treat!

▼ When you can lure the down easily, add the verbal cue, wait a few seconds to let your dog think, then lure him down to show him the association. Repeat until he'll go down on the verbal cue. Then begin using intermittent reinforcement.

Stay: What good are sit and down cues if your dog doesn't stay?

● Start with your dog in a sit or down position.

● Put the treat in front of his nose and keep it there.

● Click and reward several times while he is in position, then release him with a cue that you will always use to tell him the stay is over. Common release cues are: "all done," "break," "free," "free dog," "at ease" and "OK."

● When your Labrador Retriever will stay in sit or down position while you click and treat, add your verbal stay cue. Say "stay," pause for a second or two, click and say "stay" again. Release.

● When he's getting the idea, say "stay," whisk the treat out of sight behind your back, click, and whisk the treat back. Be sure to get it all the way to his nose, so he doesn't jump up. Gradually increase the duration of the stay.

● When your dog will stay for fifteen to twenty seconds, add small distractions: shuffling your feet, moving your arms, small hops. Increase distractions gradually. If he makes mistakes, you're adding too much, too fast.

● When he'll stay for fifteen to twenty seconds with distractions, gradually add distance. Have your dog stay, take a half-step back, click, return, and treat. When he'll stay with a half-step, tell him to stay, take a full step back, click, and return. Always return to your dog to treat after you click, but before you release. If you always return, his stay becomes strong. If you call him to you, his stay gets weaker due to his eagerness to come to you.

Come: A reliable recall—coming when called—can be a challenging behavior to teach. It is possible, however. To succeed, you need to install an automatic response to your "come" cue—one so automatic that your dog doesn't even stop to think when he hears it, but will spin on his heels and charge to you at full speed.

░ Start by charging a come cue the same way you charged your clicker. If your Lab already ignores the word "come," pick a different cue, like "front" or "hugs." Say your cue and feed him a bit of scrumptious treat. Repeat this until his eyes light up when he hears the cue. Now you're ready to start training.

░ With your dog on a leash, run away several steps and cheerfully call out your charged cue. When he follows, click the clicker. Feed him a treat when he reaches you. For a more enthusiastic come, run away at full speed as you call him. When he follows at a gallop, click, stop running, and give him a treat. The better your dog gets at coming, the farther away he can be when you call him.

░ Once your dog understands the come cue, play with more people, each with a clicker and treats. Stand a short distance apart and take turns calling and running away. Click and treat in turn as he comes to each of you. Gradually increase the distance until he comes flying to each person from a distance.

░ When you're ready to practice in wide-open spaces, attach a long line—a 20- to 50-foot leash—so you can gather up your Labrador Retriever if that taunting squirrel nearby is too much of a temptation. Then go practice where there are less tempting distractions.

Heel: Heeling means that the dog walks beside the owner without pulling. It takes time and patience on your part to succeed at teaching the dog that you will not proceed unless he is walking calmly beside him. Pulling out ahead on the leash is definitely not acceptable.

SMART TIP!

If you begin teaching the heel cue by taking long walks and letting your dog pull you along, he may misinterpret this action as an acceptable form of taking a walk. When you pull back on the leash to counteract his pulling, he will read that tug as a signal to pull even harder!

A dog who knows the basic cues is usually better behaved.

▲ Begin by holding the leash in your left hand as the dog sits beside your left leg. Move the loop end of the leash to your right hand, but keep your left hand short on the leash so that it keeps the dog close to you.

▲ Say "heel" and step forward on your left foot. Keep the dog close to you and take three steps. Stop and have the dog sit next to you in what we now call the heel position. Praise verbally, but do not touch the dog.

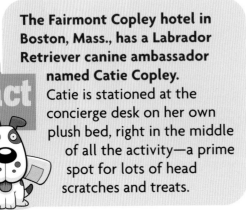

it's a Fact

The Fairmont Copley hotel in Boston, Mass., has a Labrador Retriever canine ambassador named Catie Copley. Catie is stationed at the concierge desk on her own plush bed, right in the middle of all the activity—a prime spot for lots of head scratches and treats.

Hesitate a moment and begin again with "heel," taking three steps and stopping, at which point the dog is told to sit again.

▲ Your goal here is to have the dog walk those three steps without pulling on the leash. Once he will walk calmly beside you for three steps without pulling, increase the number of steps you take to five. When he will walk politely beside you while you take five steps, you can increase the length of your walk to ten steps. Keep increasing the length of your stroll until the dog will walk quietly beside you without pulling for as long as you want him to heel. When you stop heeling, indicate to the dog that the exercise is over by petting him and saying "OK, good dog." The "OK" is used as a release word, meaning that the exercise is finished, and the dog is free to relax.

▲ If you are dealing with a dog who insists on pulling you around, simply put on your brakes and stand your ground until the dog realizes that the two of you are not

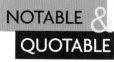
Playing games with your Lab has many benefits. It strengthens your relationship with your dog and he learns that you are the most exciting thing in his environment, so he's more likely to be attentive to you. Well-exercised dogs are also less likely to get into trouble.

—dog trainer and behavior counselor Virginia Broitman from Doswell, Va.

A well-trained, obedient and friendly dog is a joy to own.

going anywhere until he is beside you and moving at your pace, not his. It may take some time just standing there to convince the dog that you are the leader and you will be the one to decide on the direction and speed of your travel.

▲ Each time the dog looks up at you or slows down to give a slack leash between the two of you, quietly praise him and say, "Good heel. Good dog." Eventually, the dog will begin to respond, and within a few days he will be walking politely beside you without pulling on the leash. At first, the training sessions should be kept short and very positive; soon the dog will be able to walk nicely with you for increasingly longer distances. Remember to give the dog free time and the opportunity to run and play when you have finished heel practice.

TRAINING TIPS

If not properly socialized, managed, and trained, even well-bred Labs will offer raw material for undesirable behaviors such as jumping up, barking, chasing, chewing, and other destructive behaviors. You can prevent these annoying habits and help your Lab become the perfect dog you're hoping for by following some basic training and behavior tenets.

■ **Be consistent.** Consistency is important, not just in relation to what you allow your dog to do (get on the sofa, perhaps) and not do (jump up on people), but also in the verbal and body language cues you use with your dog and in his daily routine.

■ **Be gentle but firm.** Positive training methods are becoming normal. Properly applied, dog-friendly methods are wonderfully effective, creating canine-human relationships based on respect and cooperation.

■ **Manage behavior.** All living things repeat behaviors that reward them. Behaviors that aren't reinforced will go away.

■ **Provide adequate exercise.** A tired dog is a well-behaved dog. Many behavior problems can be avoided, others resolved, simply by providing your Labrador Retriever with enough exercise.

THE THREE-STEP PROGRAM

Perhaps it's too late to give your dog consistency, training, and management from the start. Maybe he came from a Lab rescue or a shelter, or you didn't realize the importance of these tenets when he was a pup. He already may have learned some bad behaviors. Perhaps they're even part of his genetic package. Many problems can be modified with ease using the following three–step process for changing an unwanted behavior.

Step No. 1: Visualize the behavior you want. If you simply try to stop your dog from

SMART TIP!

It is a good idea to enroll in an obedience class if one is available in your area. Many areas have dog clubs that offer basic obedience training as well as preparatory classes for obedience competition. There are also local dog trainers who offer similar classes.

doing something, you leave a behavior vacuum. You need to fill that vacuum with something, so your dog doesn't return to the same behavior or fill it with one that's even worse! If you're tired of your dog jumping up, decide what you'd prefer instead. A dog who greets people by sitting politely in front of them is a joy to own.

Step No. 2: Prevent your dog from being rewarded for the behavior you don't want. Management to the rescue! When your Lab jumps up to greet you or get your attention, turn your back and step away to show him that jumping up no longer works to gain attention. Step through a door, if necessary.

Step No. 3: Generously reinforce the desired behavior. Remember, dogs repeat behaviors that reward them. If Your Lab no longer gets attention for jumping up and is heavily reinforced with attention and treats for sitting, he will offer sits instead of jumping, because sits get him what he wants.

COUNTER CONDITIONING

Behaviors that respond well to the three-step process are those where the dog does something in order to get good stuff. He jumps up to get attention. He countersurfs because he finds good stuff on counters. He nips at your hands to get you to play with him.

The three steps don't work well when you're dealing with behaviors that are based in strong emotion, such as aggression and fear, or with hardwired behaviors such as chasing prey. With these, you can change the emotional or hardwired response through counter conditioning—programming a new emotional or automatic response to the stimulus by giving it a new association. Here's

When your Lab does well, praise him verbally or with treats or some extra play time.

how you would counter condition a Lab who chases after skateboarders when you're walking him on a leash.

Have a large supply of very high-value treats, such as canned chicken.

Station yourself with your Labrador on a leash at a location where skateboarders will pass by at a subthreshold distance "X"—that is, where your Lab alerts but doesn't lunge and bark.

Wait for a skateboarder. The instant your Lab notices the skateboarder, feed him bits of chicken, nonstop, until the skateboarder is gone. Stop feeding him the chicken.

Repeat many times until, when the skateboarder appears, your Lab looks at you with a big grin as if to say, "Yay! Where's my chicken?" This is a conditioned emotional response, or CER.

When you have a consistent CER at X, decrease the distance slightly, perhaps minus 1 foot, and repeat until you consistently get the CER at this distance.

Continue decreasing the distance and obtaining a CER at each level, until a skateboarder zooming right past your Labrador Retriever elicits the happy "Where's my chicken?" CER. Now go back to distance X and add a second skateboarder. Continue this process of gradual desensitization until your Lab doesn't turn a hair at a bevy of skateboarders.

CHAPTER 11

BREAKING

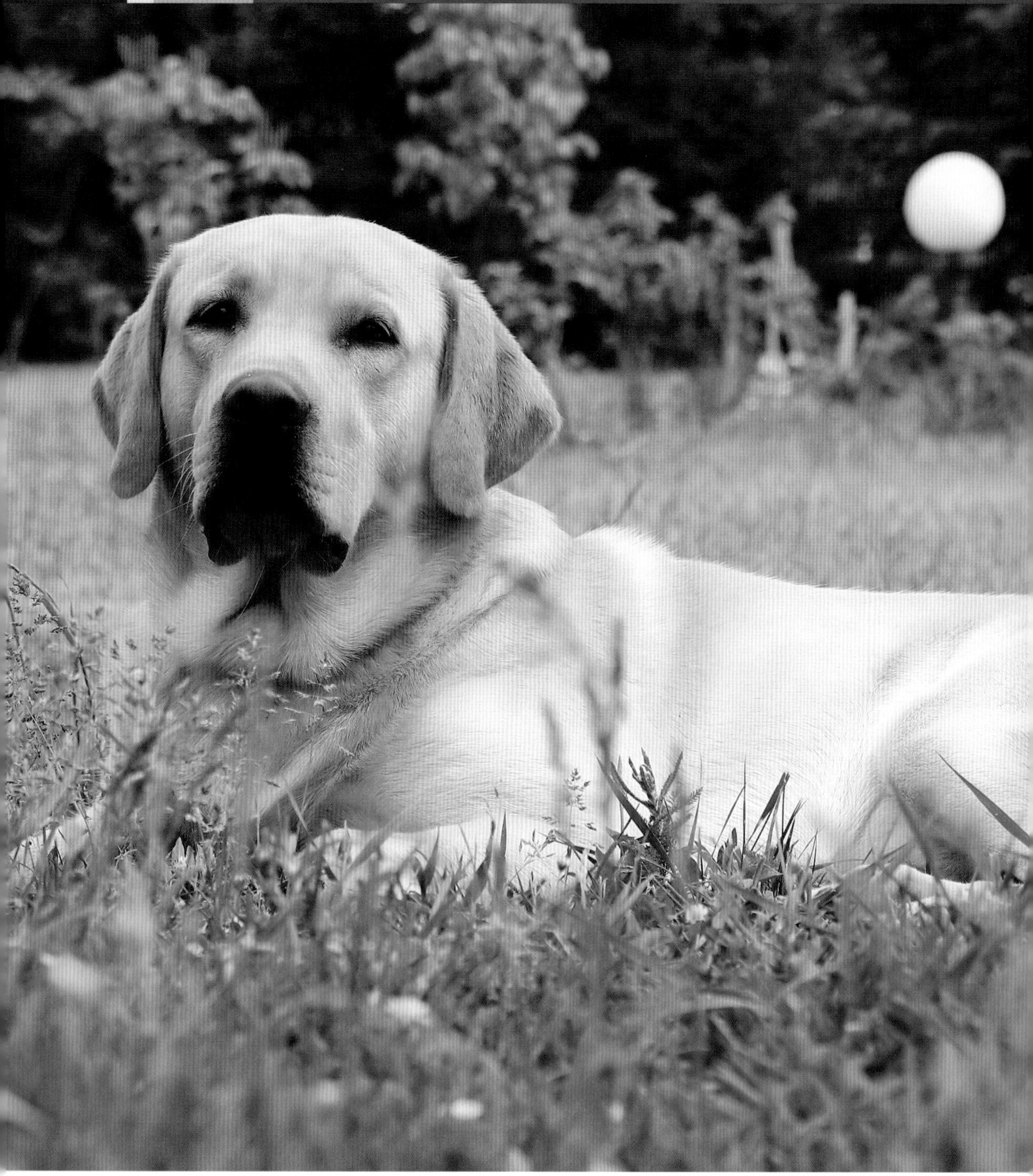

BAD HABITS

Discipline—training one to act in accordance with rules—brings order to life. It is as simple as that. Without discipline, particularly in a group society, chaos reigns supreme, and the group will eventually perish. Humans and canines are social animals and need some form of discipline in order to function effectively. Labrador Retrievers need discipline in their lives in order to understand how their pack (you and other family members) functions, and how they must act in order to survive.

The following behavioral problems are the ones that Lab owners most commonly encounter. Every dog is unique and every situation is different. Because behavioral abnormalities are the leading reason for owners' abandoning their pets, we hope that you will make a valiant effort to solve your Labrador Retriever's problems.

Did You Know?

Anxiety can make a dog miserable. Living in a world with scary, vaporous monsters and suspected retriever-eaters roaming the streets has to be pretty nerve-wracking for your Lab. The good news is that timid dogs are not doomed to be forever ruled by fear. Owners who understand a timid Lab's needs can help him build self-confidence and a more optimistic view of life.

NIP NIPPING

As puppies start to teethe, they feel the need to sink their teeth into anything—unfortunately, that includes your fingers, arms, hair, toes, whatever happens to be available. You may find this behavior cute for about the first five seconds—until you feel just how sharp those puppy teeth are. This is something you want to discourage immediately and consistently with a firm "No!" (or whatever number of firm "Nos" it takes for your dog to understand that you mean business) and replace your finger with an appropriate chew toy.

STOP THAT WHINING

A puppy will often cry, whine, whimper, howl, or make some type of commotion when he is left alone. This is basically his way of calling out for attention, of calling out to make sure that you know he is there and that you have not forgotten about him. He feels insecure when he is left alone; for example, when you are out of the house and he is in his crate, or when you are in another part of the house and he cannot see you. The noise he is making is an expression of the anxiety he feels at being alone, so he needs to be taught that being alone is OK. You are not actually training your Lab to stop making noise, you are training him to feel comfortable when he is alone and thus removing the need to make the noise.

This is where the crate with a cozy blanket and a toy come in handy. You want to know that your pup is safe when you are not there to supervise, and you know that he will be safe in his crate rather than roaming

freely about the house. In order for your Labrador Retriever to stay in his crate without making a fuss, he needs to be comfortable in his crate. On that note, it is extremely important that the crate is never used as a form of punishment, or your pup will have a negative association with the crate.

Accustom your Lab pup to the crate in short, gradually increasing intervals of time, maybe with a treat, and stay in the room with him. If he cries or makes a fuss, do not go to him, but stay in his sight. Gradually he will realize that staying in his crate is all

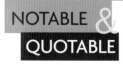

NOTABLE & QUOTABLE

An attention-seeking barking dog should get the deep freeze. If he barks, leave the room.—Victoria Schade Bresnahan, a certified pet dog trainer from Annandale, Va.

right without your help, and it will not be so traumatic for him when you are not around. You may want to leave the radio on softly when you leave the house; the sound of human voices can be comforting to him.

CHEW ON THIS

The national canine pastime is chewing! Every dog loves to sink his "canines" into a tasty bone, but most anything will do. Dogs need to chew to massage their gums, to make their new teeth feel better, and to exercise their jaws. This is a natural behavior deeply imbedded in all things canine. Our role as smart owners is not to stop the dog from chewing, but to redirect it to positive, chew-worthy objects. Be an informed owner and purchase proper chew toys for your Labrador Retriever, like strong nylon bones made for large dogs. Be sure that the devices are safe and durable because your dog's safety is at risk.

SMART TIP!

The golden rule of dog training is simple. For each "question" (cue), there is only one correct answer (reaction). One cue equals one reaction. Keep practicing the cue until your Lab reacts correctly without hesitation. Be repetitive but not monotonous. Dogs get bored just as people do; a bored dog's attention will not be focused on the lesson.

The best answer is prevention: That is, put your shoes, handbags, and other tasty objects in their proper places (out of the reach of your growing canine's mouth). Direct puppies to their toys whenever you see them tasting the furniture legs or the leg of your pants. Make a loud noise to attract your pup's attention, and immediately escort him to his chew toy and engage him with the toy for at least four minutes, praising and encouraging him all the while.

Labs are mouthy by nature, so give them a toy or ball to chew on, so they don't seek out things that may harm them.

One way to prevent digging is to always supervise your dog when he's playing outside.

CAN YOU DIG IT?

Digging, which is seen as a destructive behavior, is actually a natural instinct for dogs. Even though your Lab is not one of the "earth dogs" (also known as terriers), his desire to dig can be irrepressible and most frustrating to his owners. When digging occurs in your yard, it is actually a normal behavior redirected into something the dog can do in his everyday life.

Perhaps your dog is digging as a reaction to boredom—it is somewhat similar to someone eating a whole bag of chips in front of the television simply because they are there. Basically, the answer is to provide your dog

Did You Know?

Some natural remedies for separation anxiety are reputed to have calming effects, but check with your vet before using them. Flower essence remedies, first developed by Dr. Edward Bach, are water-based extracts of different plants, which are stabilized and preserved with brandy. A human dose is only a few drops, so seek advice from a natural healing practitioner on proper dosage for your dog.

Your Lab may howl, whine, or otherwise vocalize his displeas-
ure at your leaving the house and his being left alone. This is a
normal case of separation anxiety, but there are things that
can be done to eliminate this problem. Your dog needs to learn
that he will be fine on his own for a while and that he will not
wither away if he is not attended to every minute of the day.

In fact, constant attention can lead to separation anxiety in the first place. If you are endlessly coddling and cuddling your dog, he will come to expect this from you all the time and it will be more traumatic for him when you are not there.

One thing you can do to minimize separation anxiety is to make your entrances and exits as low-key as possible. Do not give your Lab a long, drawn-out goodbye, and do not lavish him with hugs and kisses when you return. This is giving in to the attention that he craves, and it will only make him miss it more when you are away.

Another thing you can try is to give your dog a treat when you leave; this will not keep him occupied *and* keep his mind off the fact that you just left. It will also help him associate your leaving with a pleasant experience.

You may have to accustom your Lab to being left alone in

intervals, much like when you introduced your pup to his crate. Of course, when your dog starts whimpering as you approach the door, your first instinct will be to run to him and comfort him, but don't do it! Eventually, he will adjust and be just fine if you take it in small steps. His anxiety stems from being placed in an unfamiliar situation; by familiarizing him with being alone he will learn that he is OK. That is not to say you should purposely leave your dog home alone, but your dog needs to know that while he can depend on you for his care, you do not have to be by his side 24 hours a day.

When your Lab is alone in the house, he should be confined to his crate or a designated dog-proof area of the house. This should be the area in which he sleeps, so he should already feel comfortable there, and this should make him feel more at ease when he is alone.

with adequate play and exercise so that his mind and paws are occupied, and so that he feels as if he is doing something useful.

Of course, digging is easiest to control if it is stopped as soon as possible, but it's often difficult to catch a dog in the act. One solution is to designate an area on your property where it is OK for him to dig. If you catch your Labrador Retriever digging in an off-limits area of the yard, immediately bring him to the approved area and praise him for digging there.

UNWANTED BARKING MUST GO

Barking is a dog's way of talking. It can be somewhat frustrating because it is not always easy to tell what a dog means by his bark. Is the dog excited, happy, frightened, or angry?

Whatever it is that the dog is trying to say, he should not be punished for barking. It's only when the barking becomes excessive, and when the excessive barking becomes a bad habit, that the behavior needs to be modified.

NOTABLE & QUOTABLE

Stage false departures. Pick up your car keys and put on your coat, then put them away and go about your routine. Do this several times a day, ignoring your dog while you do it. Soon his reaction to these triggers will decrease.

—September Morn, a dog trainer and behavior specialist in Bellingham, Wash.

If an intruder came into your home in the middle of the night and your dog barked a warning, wouldn't you be pleased? You probably would deem your dog a hero, a wonderful guardian, and protector of the home. On the other hand, if a friend drops by unexpectedly and rings the doorbell and is greeted with a sudden sharp bark, you probably would be annoyed at the dog. But isn't it just the same behavior? The dog doesn't know any better—unless he sees who is at the door and it's someone he's familiar with, he will bark as a means of vocalizing that his (and your) territory is being threatened. While your friend is not posing a threat, it is all the same to the dog. Barking is his means of letting you know that there is an intrusion, whether friend or foe, on your property. This type of barking is instinctive and should not be discouraged.

SMART TIP!

Do not carry your puppy to his relief area. Lead him there on a leash or, better yet, encourage him to follow you to the spot. If you start carrying him, you might end up doing this routine for months and your dog will have the satisfaction of having trained *you*.

Excessive habitual barking, however, is a problem that should be corrected early on. As your Labrador Retriever grows up, you will be able to tell when his barking is purposeful and when it is for no reason. You will be able to distinguish your dog's different barks and with what they are associated. For example, the bark when someone comes to the door will be different from the bark when he is excited to see you. It is similar to a person's tone of voice, except that the dog

Nip problem behaviors in the bud for a better-behaved dog.

has to rely totally on tone of voice because he does not have the benefit of using words. An incessant barker will be evident at an early age.

There are some things that encourage a dog to bark. For example, if your dog barks nonstop for a few minutes and you give him a treat to quiet him, he believes that you are rewarding him for barking. He will associate barking with getting a treat, and will keep doing it until he is rewarded.

NO MORE JUMPING

Jumping up is a dog's friendly way of saying hello! Some dog owners do not mind when their dog jumps up, which is fine for

them. The problem arises when guests come to the house, and the dog greets them in the same manner—whether they like it or not! However friendly the greeting may be, chances are your visitors will not appreciate nearly being knocked over by sixty or more pounds of Lab. The dog will not be able to distinguish upon whom he can jump and whom he cannot. Therefore, it is probably best to discourage this behavior entirely.

Pick a cue such as "Off!" (avoid using "down" because you will use that for your dog to lie down) when he jumps up. Place him on the ground on all fours and have him sit, praising him the whole time. Always lavish him with praise and petting when he is in the sit position. That way you are still giving him a warm, affectionate greeting, because you are as excited to see him as he is to see you!

STOP FOOD STEALING AND BEGGING

Is your dog devising ways of stealing food from your countertops? If so, you must answer the following questions: Is your Labrador Retriever hungry, or is he constantly famished like every other chowhound? Why is there food on the countertop? Face it, some dogs are more food-motivated than others; some dogs are totally obsessed by a slab of brisket and can only think of their next meal. To them, food steal-

ing is terrific fun and always yields a great reward—food, glorious food!

The smart owner's goal, therefore, is to make the "reward" less rewarding, even startling! Plant a shaker can (an empty can with coins inside) on the counter so that it catches your pooch off-guard. There are other devices available that will surprise your dog when he is looking for a mid-afternoon snack. Such remote-control devices, though not the first choice of some trainers, allow the correction to come from the object instead of the owner. These devices are also useful to keep the snacking dog from napping on furniture that is forbidden.

Just like food stealing, begging is a favorite pastime of hungry puppies with that same reward—food! Dogs quickly learn that their owners keep the "good food" for themselves, and that we humans do not dine on kibble alone. Begging is a conditioned response related to a specific stimulus, time, and place. The sounds of the kitchen, cans and bottles opening, crinkling bags,

and the smell of food in preparation will excite your chowhound and soon the paws are in the air!

Here is the solution to stopping this behavior: Never give in to a Labrador beggar! You are rewarding the dog for sitting pretty, jumping up, whining, and rubbing his nose into you by giving him that glorious reward—food. By ignoring your dog, you will (eventually) force the behavior into extinction. Note that the behavior likely gets worse before it disappears, so be sure there aren't any softies in the family who will give in to your Labrador Retriever every time he whimpers, "More, please."

YUCK!

Feces eating, aka coprophagia, one of the most disgusting behaviors a dog could engage in, yet to the dog it is perfectly nor-

NOTABLE & QUOTABLE *The purpose of puppy classes is for the pups to learn how to learn. The pups get the training along the way, but the training is almost secondary.*

—*professional trainer Peggy Shunick Duezabou of Helena, Mont.*

mal. Vets have found that diets with low digestibility, containing relatively low levels of fiber and high levels of starch, increase coprophagia. Therefore, high-fiber diets may decrease the likelihood of dogs eating feces. To discourage this behavior, feed food that is nutritionally complete and in the proper amount. If changes in the diet do not work, and no medical cause can be found, you will have to modify the behavior through environmental control before it becomes a habit.

There are tricks you can try, such as adding an unpleasant-tasting substance to the feces to make it unpalatable or adding something to the dog's food that will make it unpleasant tasting after it passes through the dog. The best way to prevent him from eating his stool is to make it unavailable; clean up after he eliminates and remove any stool

SMART TIP!

Do not have long practice sessions with your Labrador. He will become easily bored if you do. Also: Never practice when you are tired, ill, worried, or in a negative mood. This will transmit to your Lab and may have an adverse effect on his performance.

from the yard. If it is not there, he can't eat it.

Never reprimand your dog for stool eating, as this rarely works. Vets recommend distracting your dog while he is in the act of eating feces. Another option is to muzzle him when he is in the yard to relieve himself; this usually is effective within thirty to sixty days. Coprophagia most frequently is seen in pups six to twelve months of age, and usually disappears around the dog's first birthday.

SPORTING DOGS

All dogs require some form of exercise, regardless of breed. A sedentary lifestyle is as harmful to a dog as it is to a person. The Labrador Retriever happens to be an active breed that requires considerable exercise, but you don't have to be a weightlifter or marathon runner to provide your dog with the exercise he needs.

Regular walks, play sessions in the yard, or letting your dog run free in the fenced yard under your supervision are all sufficient forms of exercise for a Labrador Retriever. For those who are more ambitious, you will find that your Lab will be able to keep up with you on extra-long walks, the morning run, or, of course, a swim.

Not only is exercise essential to keep your dog's body fit, it is essential to his mental well-being, too. A bored dog will find something to do, which often manifests itself in some type of destructive behavior. In this sense, it is essential for the smart owner's mental well-being, as well!

Walking is just as beneficial for Labradors as it is for humans. A brisk walk of a reasonable distance is still the best way to exercise his lungs and limbs. Moreover, the human walker will also reap the health benefits of regular exercise.

it's a Fact

The **Fédération Internationale Cynologique** is the world **kennel club** that governs dog shows in Europe and elsewhere around the world.

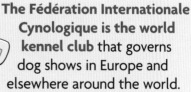

Before You Begin
Because of the physical demands of sporting activities, a Lab puppy shouldn't officially begin training until he is done growing. That doesn't mean, though, that you can't begin socializing him to sports. Talk to your vet about what age is appropriate.

Games in which your dog fetches items such as a ball or a Frisbee are also excellent ways to exercise. As you teach your Lab to fetch, remember that he's a predator at heart and he instinctively loves to chase things. To him, a ball or disc is just as exciting as a real rabbit, provided that it's moving and he can catch it. Be sure to praise lavishly when he does, so he will be anxious to do it again and again.

If you really want to get sporty, try some of the several organized activities that Labradors do well in and enjoy, such as field trials, tracking, hunting programs, obedience, agility, rally, conformation, flyball, and dock jumping.

FIELD TRIALS

Field trials are offered to the retrievers, pointers, and spaniel breeds of the Sporting Group, as well as to Beagles and Bassets of the Hound Group. The purpose of field trials is to demonstrate a dog's ability to perform his original purpose in the field. The events vary depending on the type of dog, but in all trials dogs compete against one another for placement and for points toward their Field Champion titles.

Retriever field trials, designed to simulate "an ordinary day's shoot," are popular and

Labs excel at dog sports, especially Frisbee.

likely the most demanding of these trials. Dogs are tested both on land and water. Difficulty levels are based on the number of birds downed as well as the number of "blind retrieves" (where a bird is placed away from the view of the dog, and the handler directs the dog by the use of hand signals and verbal cues). Every trial includes four stakes of increasing levels of difficulty. Each stake is judged by a team of two judges who look for many natural abilities including steadiness, courage, style, control, and training.

TRACKING

Would you prefer a quiet, peaceful sport for your Lab's instinctive talents? How about the investigative sport of tracking? Labradors are known for their keen sense of smell, which makes tracking a natural activity for them. Their coat allows them to go through tough terrain and not get tangled in rose or burr bushes, and they're not afraid to plunge into the heaviest cover to follow a track.

As the owner of a sporting breed, you no doubt recognize the incredible olfactory ability that enables a dog to detect downed birds in an icy lake. The American Kennel Club sport of tracking similarly utilizes this remarkable faculty, asking your dog to locate and follow a human scent trail with the approved age, length, and number of turns per the competition level. Titles are based on

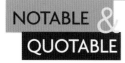

For a dog to be considered for field work, he needs to love retrieving and being trained, even when you ask him for things he doesn't like. Hunt tests and field trials require a genuine enjoyment of looking for birds, picking up birds and returning birds to their handlers.

—Julie Knutson, field trial and hunt-test trainer of Gunclub Labradors in Orchard, Colo.

the type of surface covered, ranging from rough, rural ground to urban landscape, such as pavement and gravel.

Your Lab must also indicate articles dropped along the track by picking the item up, lying down, or performing another consistently identifiable behavior. Initial tests are limited to a glove or wallet, but advanced levels include other small objects.

Start teaching your Lab this sport by encouraging him to find objects using scent. You can start with treats and work up to other objects. Get help by joining a tracking class, which will get you started on the right path to training your dog.

HUNTING TRIALS

Hunting tests are not competitive like field trials, and participating dogs are judged against a standard like in a conformation show. The first hunting tests were devised by the North American Hunting Retriever Association as an alternative to field trials for retriever owners to appreciate their dogs'

innate ability in the field without the expense and pressure of a formal field trial. The intent of hunting tests is the same as that of field trials: to test the dog's ability in a simulated hunting scenario.

The AKC instituted its hunting tests in 1985, and since then popularity has grown tremendously. In addition to the AKC, the United Kennel Club also offers hunting tests through its affiliate club, the Hunting Retriever Club Inc., which began the tests in 1984.

AGILITY TRIALS

Agility is one of the most popular dog sports out there. Labradors are excellent at this activity, which requires speed, precision, and obedience. Training your Labrador in agility will boost his confidence and teach him to focus on you.

In agility competition, the dog and handler move through a prescribed course, negotiating a series of obstacles that may include jumps, tunnels, an A-frame, a seesaw, a dog walk, a pause table, and weave

Agility is a fun sport that will challenge your dog mentally and otherwise.

poles. Dogs who run through a course without refusing any obstacles, going off course or knocking down any bars, all within a set time, get a qualifying score. Dogs with a certain number of qualifying scores in their given division (Novice, Open, Excellent, and Mach, at AKC trials) earn an agility title.

Several organizations recognize agility events. AKC-sanctioned events are the most common. The United States Dog Agility Association also sanctions trials, as does the UKC. The rules are different for each organization, but the principles are the same.

OBEDIENCE TRIALS

Obedience trials in the United States trace back to the early 1930s, when organized obedience training was developed to demonstrate how well the dog and owner could work together. The pioneer of obedience trials is Helen Whitehouse Walker, a Standard Poodle fancier, who designed a series of exercises after the Associated Sheep, Police Army Dog Society of Great Britain. Since the days of Walker, obedience trials have grown by leaps and bounds, and today there are over 2,000 trials held in the United States every year, with more than 100,000 dogs competing. Any registered AKC or ILP (Indefinite Listing Privilege) dog can enter an obedience trial, regardless of conformational disqualifications or neutering.

Obedience trials are divided into three levels of progressive difficulty. At the first level, Novice, dogs compete for the title

For your dog to compete well in obedience, he would need to know the basic cues first (sit, stay, lie down, come).

Companion Dog; at the intermediate level, Open, dogs compete for the title Companion Dog Excellent; and at the advanced level, dogs compete for the title Utility Dog. Classes are subdivided into "A" (for beginners) and "B" (for more experienced handlers). A perfect score at any level is 200, and a dog must score 170 or better to earn a "leg," of which three are needed to earn the title. To earn points, the dog must score more than fifty percent of the available points in each exercise; the possible points range from twenty to forty.

Once a dog has earned the UD title, he can compete with other proven obedience dogs for the coveted title of Utility Dog Excellent, which requires that the dog win "legs" in ten shows. In 1977, the title Obedience Trial Champion was established by the AKC. Utility Dogs who earn "legs" in Open B and Utility B earn points toward their Obedience Trial Champion title. To become an OTCh., a dog needs to earn 100 points, which requires three first-place wins in Open B and Utility under three different judges.

The Grand Prix of obedience trials, the AKC National Obedience Invitational, gives qualifying Utility Dogs the chance to win the newest and highest title: National Obedience Champion. Only the top twenty-five ranked obedience dogs, plus any dog ranked in the top three in his breed, can compete.

RALLY BEHIND RALLY

Rally is a sport that combines competition obedience with elements of agility, but is

NOTABLE & QUOTABLE

I like how flyball forces me to watch my Lab's weight and keep him in shape. It's partly why he still acts like a two-year-old at the age of seven, when too many Labs I know are slow and overweight by age five.—flyball enthusiast Jill Miller, a training instructor in Madison, Wis.

less demanding than either one of these activities. The sport was designed for the average dog owner, and is easier than many other sporting activities.

At a rally event, dogs and handlers are asked to move through ten to twenty stations, depending on the level of competition. The stations are marked by numbered signs, which tell the handler the exercise to be performed at this station. The exercises vary from making different types of turns to changing pace.

Dogs can earn rally titles as they get better at the sport and move through the different levels. The titles to strive for are Rally Novice, Rally Advanced, Rally Excellent, and Rally Advanced Excellent.

To get your Labrador Retriever prepared for rally competition, focus on teaching basic obedience, for starters. Your dog must know the five basic obedience cues and perform them well before he's ready for rally. Next,

you can enroll your dog in a rally class. Although he must be at least six months of age to compete in rally, you can start training long before his six-month birthday.

SHOW DOGS

When you purchase your Labrador Retriever, you will make it clear to the breeder whether you want one just as a lovable companion and pet, or if you hope to buy a Labrador with show prospects. No reputable breeder will sell you a young puppy and tell you that he is definitely of show quality, for so much can go wrong during the early months of a puppy's development. If you plan to show, what you will hopefully have acquired is a puppy with "show potential."

To the novice, exhibiting a Labrador Retriever in the show ring may look easy, but it takes a lot of hard work and devotion to compete at a show such as the

Westminster Kennel Club dog show, not to mention a little luck, too!

The first concept that the canine novice learns when watching a dog show is that each dog first competes against members of his own breed. Once the judge has selected the best member of each breed (Best of Breed), the chosen dog will compete with other dogs in his group. Finally, the dogs chosen first in each of the seven groups will compete for Best in Show.

The second concept that you must understand is that the dogs are not actually compared against one another. The judge compares each dog against the breed standard, the written description of the ideal specimen that is approved by the AKC. While some early breed standards were based on specific dogs that were famous or popular, many dedicated enthusiasts say that a perfect speci-

SMART TIP!

Before You Begin
Sports are demanding physically. Have your vet do a full examination of your Labrador Retriever to rule out joint problems, heart disease, eye aliments, and other maladies. Once you get the all-clear healthwise, start having fun in your new sporting life!

men, as described in the standard, has never walked into a show ring, has never been bred and, to the woe of dog breeders around the globe, does not exist. Breeders attempt to get as close to this ideal as possible with every litter. (And if the "perfect" dog were born, breeders and judges probably would never agree that it was indeed perfect.)

If you are interested in exploring the world of conformation, your best bet is to join your local breed club or the national

(or parent) club, which is the Labrador Retriever Club of America. These clubs often host both regional and national specialties, shows only for Labrador Retrievers, which can include conformation as well as obedience and field trials. Even if you have no intention of competing with your Labrador, a specialty is like a festival for lovers of the breed who congregate to share their favorite topic: Labrador Retrievers! Clubs also send out newsletters, and some organize training days and seminars in order that people may learn more about their chosen breed. To locate the breed club closest to you, contact the AKC, which furnishes the rules and regulations for all of these events, plus general dog registration and other basic requirements of dog ownership.

FLYBALL

Fast and intense, flyball consists of four consecutive hurdles set at a height appropriate for the shortest dog on the team. Just beyond the hurdles sits every retriever's dream machine—a spring-loaded box that ejects a tennis ball at the push of a pedal. For competition, each member of the four-dog team must leap the hurdles, jump on the release pedal, catch the resultant ball and repeat his path back to the waiting handler, allowing the next dog to begin.

An athletic sport that revolves around catching and carrying tennis balls while racing other dogs promises tremendous fun for a fanatic fetcher like the Labrador Retriever, often prompting participants to voice their excitement.

Obviously, with racing, jumping, and impacting a stationary object, the Lab's stocky physique warrants a few concerns, particularly when "hitting" the box.

Approached with common sense, flyball represents a wonderful pursuit for dog and handler. Less common than agility, flyball classes can be difficult to find. Ask fellow trainers if they know of anyone active in flyball willing to work with a newcomer. Another option is to contact the North American Flyball Association, the ruling organization that bestows flyball titles and maintains breed statistics, for information on a local club or, if necessary, how to start one yourself.

Did You Know?

In musical freestyle (also known as freestyle obedience or dancing with dogs), you and your Lab can dance your way to a title. There are two major sanctioning organizations for musical freestyle competitions, the World Canine Freestyle Organization and the Canine Freestyle Federation.

BIG AIR OR DOCKDOGS

Popularized by television's ESPN Great Outdoor Games, Big Air competitions have rapidly gained favor among audiences and competitors alike, as dogs create "hang time" after launching off a dock to retrieve a toy or dummy thrown into the water. The governing organization, DockDogs, was formed in 2000 to establish specific rules and standards, as well as to promote Big Air as a viable, enjoyable canine sport.

For competition, the dock must measure 40 feet long, 8 feet wide and rest 2 feet off the water's surface. The dock is covered with a rubbery material or carpeting for safe footing for running and take-off. To encourage the dog to jump as far as possible, the handler throws a chase object into the water. Jumps are digitally measured from the end of the dock to the point where the dog's rump breaks the water.

Considering the Labrador Retriever's history in water retrieval work, it's no surprise that Labs enjoy the sport, as do their owners. Many clubs exist across the country.

Dean Skillman and his yellow Lab, Wylie (both pictured), participate in—and dominate—dock jumping competitions.

Courtesy of Dean Skillman

Dean Skillman of Lambertville, Mich., enjoys hunting, and having owned Labs in the past, he thought that his yellow Lab, Wylie, might also make a good hunting companion, which he did.

But early on, Skillman recognized that there was something different about this dog, something that went a bit beyond any Labrador he'd ever worked with. "Wylie was eleven months old," Skillman recounts, "and we were standing by the pool, and I was throwing him the ball." He threw the ball over the pool, expecting Wylie to run around the pool to fetch it, but instead Wylie launched himself over the water to catch the ball! Skillman was in shock at what he'd just seen.

"So I threw the ball eight or nine more times [over the water]," he says. Every time, Wylie catapulted himself into the air, caught the ball and splashed into the pool.

He and Wylie entered their first DockDogs Big Air competition in January 2004. The Big Air competition measures the distance the dog jumps from the edge of the dock to the point of entry into the water at the base of the dog's tail.

Just how far did Wylie go on his first attempt? "A lot of dogs are natural jumpers and they'll go 20 feet their first time," Skillman says. "Wylie's first jump was only 8 feet." But, Wylie improved, in leaps and bounds, literally. He finished his first season with a second-place finish in the first DockDogs National Championships in October 2004, eventually crossing 26 feet, 6 inches.

Just four years after beginning the sport, Wylie's *curriculum vitae* reads like a "Who's Who" of DockDogs events. His personal best for the DockDogs Extreme Vertical event, which measures the height to which a dog can jump to grab a bumper (a soft, buoyant, sausage-shaped fetch toy) suspended above the pool, is 7 feet, 2 inches. And then there's Speed Retrieve, an event that times how long it takes for a dog to jump, swim, and fetch a bumper that has been placed 52 feet from the edge of the dock. Wylie set the world record in 2008 with a time of 6.21 seconds, and then beat his own record a few months later with a blistering 5.37 seconds!

For more information about the Labrador Retriever, contact the following organizations. They will be more than happy to help you fetch what you are looking for.

AMERICAN KENNEL CLUB: The AKC website offers information and links to conformation, tracking, rally, obedience, agility programs, and member clubs: www.akc.org

CANADIAN KENNEL CLUB: Our northern neighbor's oldest kennel club is similar to the AKC and the UKC in America. www.ckc.ca

CANINE FREESTYLE FEDERATION: Learn more about dancing with your dog. www.canine-freestyle.org

CANINE PERFORMANCE EVENTS: Get your Lab started in agility. www.k9cpe.com

DockDogs: Labradors love water, which makes them natural dock jumpers! www.dockdogs.com

HUNTING RETRIEVER CLUB INC: This is an international club for hunters. www.hrc-ukc.com

LABRADOR RETRIEVER CLUB: This is the national AKC-sanctioned Lab club. www.thelabradorclub.com

LABRADOR RETRIEVER RESCUE: This nonprofit volunteer organization is dedicated to rescuing and placing abandoned Labs. www.lrr.org

NORTH AMERICAN DOG AGILITY COUNCIL: This site provides links to clubs, trainers, and agility trainers in the United States and Canada: www.nadac.com

NORTH AMERICAN FLYBALL ASSOCIATION: Get together a team of local dogs and start playing. www.flyball.org

**NORTH AMERICAN HUNTING RE-
TRIEVER ASSOCIATION:** Get in the hunt.
www.nahranews.net

UNITED KENNEL CLUB: The UKC offers
several of the events offered by the AKC, including agility, conformation, and obedience.
In addition, the UKC offers competitions in
hunting and dog sport (companion and protective events). Both the UKC and the AKC
offer programs for juniors, ages two to eighteen: www.ukcdogs.com

**UNITED STATES DOG AGILITY
ASSOCIATION:** The USDAA has information on training, clubs, and events in the
United States, Canada, Mexico, and over-
seas: www.usdaa.com

**WORLD CANINE FREESTYLE ORGANI-
ZATION:** You can dance with your Labrador
Retriever in choreographed musical programs performed by handlers and their
dogs in this fun and exciting new sport.
www.worldcaninefreestyle.org

BOARDING

So you want to take a family vacation—and you want to include all members of the family. You probably would make arrangements for accommodations ahead of time anyway, but this is especially important when traveling with a dog. You do not want to make an overnight stop at the only place around for miles and find out that they do not allow dogs. Also, you do not want to reserve a room for your family without confirming that you are traveling with a dog because, if it is against their policy, you may not have a place to stay.

Alternatively, if you are traveling and choose not to bring your Lab, you will have to arrange accommodations for him. Some options are to bring him to a neighbor's house, to have a trusted neighbor stop by often or stay at your house, or to bring your dog to a reputable boarding kennel.

If you choose to board him at a kennel, you should visit in advance to see the facili-

ties and check how clean they are and where the dogs are kept. Talk to some of the employees and see how they treat the dogs—do they spend time with the dogs, play with them, exercise them, etc.? Also, find out the kennel's policy on vaccinations and what they require. This is for all of the dogs' safety because when dogs are kept together, there is a greater risk of diseases being passed from dog to dog.

HOME STAFFING

For the Lab parent who works all day, a pet sitter or dog walker may be the perfect solution for a lonely Lab longing for a midday stroll. Smart dog owners can approach local high schools or community centers if they don't know a neighbor who's interested in a part-time commitment. Interview potential dog walkers and consider their experience with dogs and your Labrador's rapport with the candidate. Always check references before entrusting your dog and home to a new dog walker.

For an owner's long-term absence, such as a three-day business trip or a vacation, many Lab owners welcome the services of a pet-sitter. It's usually less stressful on the dog to stay home with a pet sitter than to be boarded in a kennel. Pet sitters also may be more affordable than a week's stay at a full-service doggie day care.

Pet sitters must be even more reliable than dog walkers, as the dog is depending on his surrogate owner for all of his needs for an extended period of time. Owners should hire a certified pet sitter through the National Association of Professional Pet Sitters, which can be accessed online at www.petsitters.org. NAPPS provides pet sitter locator services. The nonprofit organization only certifies serious-minded, professionals who are knowledgeable in behavior, nutrition, health, and safety. Always keep your Lab's best interest at heart when planning a trip.

SMART TIP!

Remember to keep your dog's leash slack when interacting with other dogs. It is not unusual for a dog to pick out one or two canine neighbors to dislike. If you know there's bad blood between your dog and an oncoming dog, step off to the side and put a barrier, such as a parked car, between the dogs. If there are no barriers around, move to the side of the walkway, cue your dog to sit, stay, and watch you until his nemesis passes; then continue your walk.

SCHOOL'S IN SESSION

Puppy kindergarten, which is usually open to puppies between three and six months of age, allows puppies to learn and socialize with other dogs and people in a structured setting. Classes help your Lab enjoy going places with you, and help your dog become a well-behaved member of public gatherings that include other dogs. They prepare him for adult obedience classes, as well as for life.

The problem with most puppy kindergarten classes is that they only occur one night a week. What do you do about the rest of the week?

If you're at home all week, you may be able to find other places to take your puppy, but you have to be careful about dog parks and locations where just any dog can go. An experience with a bully can undo all the good your classes have done, or worse, end in tragedy.

If you work, your puppy may be home alone all day, a tough situation for an energetic Labrador Retriever. Chances are he can't hold himself that long, so your potty training will be undermined unless you're just aiming to teach him to use an indoor potty. And chances are, by the time you come home, he'll be bursting with energy that you may start feeling that he's hyperactive.

The answer? Doggie day care. Most larger cities have some sort of day care, whether it's a boarding kennel that keeps your dog in a run or a full-service day care that offers training, play time, and even spa facilities. They range from a person who keeps a few dogs at his home to a state-of-the-art facility built just for dogs. Many of the more sophisticated doggie day cares offer webcams so you can see your dog throughout the day.

Look for:
- escape-proof facilities, including a buffer between the dogs and any doors
- inoculation requirements for incoming dogs
- midday meals for young dogs
- obedience training (if offered), using reward-based methods
- safe and comfortable time-out areas for sleeping
- screening of dogs for aggression
- small playgroups of similar sizes and ages
- toys and playground equipment, such as tunnels
- trained staff, with an adequate number to supervise the dogs (no more than ten to fifteen dogs per person)
- a webcam

Puppy classes will teach your Lab to get along with other dogs.

CAR TRAVEL

You should accustom your Lab to riding in a car at an early age. You may or may not take him in the car often, but at the very least he will need to go to the vet, and you do not want these trips to be traumatic for your Lab or troublesome for you. The safest way for a dog to ride in the car is in his crate. If he uses a crate in the house, you can use the same crate for travel.

Another option is a specially made safety harness for dogs, which straps the dog in much like a seat belt. Do not let your dog roam loose in the vehicle—this is very dangerous! If you should stop short, your dog can be thrown and injured. If your Lab starts climbing on you and pestering you while you are driving, you will not be able to concentrate on the road. It's an unsafe situation for everyone—human and canine.

For long trips, be prepared to stop to let your dog relieve himself. Take with you whatever you need to clean up after him, including some paper towels and perhaps some old bath towels for use should he have an accident in the car or suffer from motion sickness.

Did You Know? **A dog run is one of the few urban spaces where a dog can be off-leash.** To enter most dog parks, dogs must be fully vaccinated and healthy, and females must not be in season.

IDENTIFICATION

Your Labrador Retriever is your valued companion and friend. That is why you always keep a close eye on him and you have made sure that he cannot escape from the yard or wriggle out of his collar and run away from you. However, accidents can happen and there may come a time when your dog unexpectedly gets separated from you. If this unfortunate event should occur, the first thing on your mind will be finding him. Proper identification, including an ID tag, a tattoo, and possibly a microchip, will increase the chances of his being returned to you safely and quickly.

An ID tag on a collar or harness is the primary means of pet identification (and ID licenses are required in many communities, anyway). Although inexpensive and easy to read, collars and ID tags can come off or be taken off.

A microchip doesn't get lost. Containing a unique ID number that can be read by a scanner, the microchip is embedded under the pet's skin. It's invaluable for identifying lost or stolen pets. However, to be effective, the chip must be registered with a national database and owner contact info kept up to date. Additionally, not every shelter or veterinary clinic has a scanner, nor do most folks who might pick up and try to return the lost pet. Best bet: Get both!

Did You Know? Some communities have created regular dog runs and separate spaces for small dogs. These small-dog runs are ideal for introducing puppies to the dog park experience. The runs are smaller, the participants are smaller, and their owners are often more vigilant because they are used to watching out for their fragile companions.